FACING
THE
MOUNTAIN

A True Story of Japanese American
Heroes in World War II

DANIEL JAMES BROWN

VIKING

FOR KATS, RUDY, FRED, AND GORDON

VIKING
An imprint of Penguin Random House LLC, New York

First published in the United States of America by Viking,
an imprint of Penguin Random House LLC, 2023

Visit us online at PenguinRandomHouse.com.

Library of Congress Cataloging-in-Publication Data is available.

ISBN 9780593465660

1st Printing

Printed in the United States of America

LSCH

Edited by Kelsey Murphy
Design by Lily Qian
Text set in Charter

This is a work of nonfiction. Some names and identifying details have been changed.

ALSO BY DANIEL JAMES BROWN

The Boys in the Boat:
The True Story of an American Team's Epic Journey to Win
Gold at the 1936 Olympics
(Young Readers Adaptation)

FOR ADULTS:

Under a Flaming Sky:
The Great Hinckley Firestorm of 1894

The Indifferent Stars Above:
The Harrowing Saga of a Donner Party Bride

The Boys in the Boat:
Nine Americans and Their Epic Quest for Gold at the 1936
Berlin Olympics

Facing the Mountain:
A True Story of Japanese American Heroes in
World War II

CONTENTS

A WORD ABOUT WORDS

TO TELL AN HONEST STORY, a writer must use honest words. As you read this book, I hope you will keep that fact in mind. I certainly have as I have written it.

I mention this for several reasons. For one thing, many of the words that have been used for years to talk about the history described in this book are words that were designed to be deliberately dishonest. When the US government announced that tens of thousands of Japanese Americans were to be forcibly removed from their homes, military and political leaders called this an "evacuation." They called the fairgrounds and racetracks where Japanese Americans were first confined behind barbed wire "assembly centers." They called the process of rounding them up and incarcerating them "internment." They called the permanent camps to which Japanese Americans were later moved and where they were held against their will "relocation centers." All of these words were chosen to make what was happening to Japanese Americans sound more acceptable to the American public.

I want to call particular attention to that last term. These camps were not "relocation centers." They were concentration camps. They were created to concentrate Japanese Americans, based entirely on their race, behind barbed wire in order to separate them from other Americans. So I sometimes refer to the camps with this term.

At the same time, it's important to underscore that in using the term "concentration camps" I do not mean to compare these American camps to the horrific death camps and slave-labor camps created by the Nazis in Germany and Poland during World War II. Those Nazi camps—places like Dachau and Auschwitz-Birkenau—represent an evil that is beyond all imagining.

Another part of using language honestly means recognizing when it is racist. In reading this book, you will occasionally encounter the word "Jap." It is a racist term, widely used by millions of Americans during the period of history this book discusses. It was used to hurt and demean both Japanese citizens and Japanese Americans, just as the N-word has been used to hurt and demean African Americans and other Black people. It has no place in our society, a society created on the idea, and the fact, that all people are created equal. It appears in this book only for the purpose of showing honestly how deeply rooted racism against Japanese Americans was during this time in history.

CHAPTER 1

—✕—✕—✕—✕—✕—✕—✕—

ON THE BEACH AT WAIKĪKĪ, swimmers lay towels on the soft, coral sand and waded into the turquoise surf. Coffee percolated in sunny kitchens, the yellow blossoms of hau trees opened, and mynah birds chattered in the palm trees. All across the island of Oʻahu, people went about the business of greeting another beautiful Hawaiian day—December 7, 1941.

At first, they looked like swarms of insects drifting across the pale, early morning sky. Then they looped around the mountains and spiraled down, in groups of five or six. US Navy and Army personnel and civilians alike stopped what they were doing and peered at the sky, all wondering the same thing. *What on earth was this?*

The gray steel and roaring engines of the Japanese warplanes drew nearer. At 7:48 a.m., they struck Kāneʻohe Bay Naval Air Station, raking the parked aircraft with machine-gun fire, setting them ablaze. Then they circled back through billowing clouds of black smoke, strafing anything in their path: cars racing toward the scene, men scrambling to find cover, even private homes. About seven minutes later, planes struck other airfields on O'ahu. Within minutes, the United States' capability to mount an air defense vanished in a maelstrom of flames, shattered glass, and twisted metal.

Then the attackers wheeled their planes around and turned to Pearl Harbor, where seven battleships were lined up alongside Ford Island and an eighth was sitting helpless in dry dock. On the USS *Nevada*, a military band was striking up "The Star-Spangled Banner" for the 8:00 a.m. ceremony of raising the American flag. A Japanese bomber roared in and sprayed machine-gun fire across the deck, somehow missing the musicians but shredding the flag halfway up the pole. The band kept playing until the anthem was finished. Then, flinging their instruments aside, they scrambled for cover.

On the USS *Oklahoma*, a sailor roared, "Man your battle stations!"[1] At that very moment, two torpedoes punched into the ship's side, and it began to list. Then a third torpedo hit, and the ship rolled over, trapping hundreds belowdecks. Its great gray hull lay turned to the sky like the belly of a dead whale.

At about the same time, seven torpedoes and two aerial bombs hit the USS *West Virginia*, trapping another sixty-six men belowdecks. Within minutes, all eight battleships and a number of other ships had been hit.

Then the worst of it: An armor-piercing bomb penetrated the foredeck of the USS *Arizona* and detonated perhaps a million pounds of explosives stored in its forward hold.

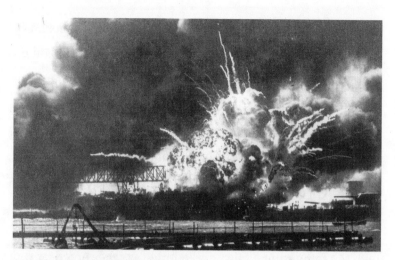

THE USS *SHAW* EXPLODES DURING THE ATTACK ON PEARL HARBOR.

A fireball engulfed the ship, and a shock wave pulsed out across Pearl Harbor. Within moments, 1,177 of its crew were dead—nearly half the total death toll for the day.

A second wave of 167 planes was now bearing down on the island, and a deadly hailstorm of Japanese bombs and misdirected US antiaircraft shells fell on residential areas, setting houses on fire, crumpling cars, and taking forty-nine civilian lives.

The planes flew so low that people on the ground could see the faces of the pilots—sometimes stone-faced, sometimes grinning, sometimes even waving as they passed overhead. And those pilots, looking down, must have noticed that many of the faces staring back up at them in astonishment were very like the faces back home in Japan.

In 1941, nearly a third of Hawai'i's residents were of

Japanese ancestry. In the 1830s, the islands were colonized by white missionaries who established sugarcane and pineapple plantations. Initially, they employed the Native Hawaiians, but there were too few of them to meet the needs of the sprawling plantations. So the planters, and their descendants, began to import labor. The workers were mostly from East Asia—China, the Philippines, Korea, and Japan. By far the largest group was the Japanese. As the horrors of that December day unfolded, these Japanese residents, and their American children, reacted with the same stunned fury and outrage as other Americans.

Seventeen-year-old Daniel Inouye was getting dressed, listening idly to Hawaiian music on the radio, when the announcer, Webley Edwards, broke in with a bulletin, screaming into the mic—"This is no test! This is the real McCoy! Pearl Harbor is being bombed by the Japanese! Get off the streets!"[2]

Defying the broadcaster's advice, Inouye rushed from his house in Honolulu's Mōʻiliʻili neighborhood. He saw the Rising Sun insignia—the Japanese national emblem—on the wings of a Zero passing overhead and was immediately overwhelmed by a wave of anger and dread. "I thought my life had come to an end," he later said.[3] But he got on his bike and raced to a first aid station at a nearby elementary school, where he spent most of the next three days and nights helping treat the wounded and carrying the dead to the morgue.

Katsugo "Kats" Miho was also getting ready for the day, shaving in his room at his university dorm, when a commotion erupted downstairs—a bunch of fellows yelling, heavy footsteps running down the stairs. Curious, he leaned over a banister and shouted down the stairwell, "What's going on down there?"

Someone shouted back, "Put on the radio!"

Someone else yelled, "We're being attacked!"[4]

When Kats turned on the radio, an announcer was screaming something about Pearl Harbor. Kats scrambled

A CIVILIAN HOME DAMAGED DURING THE PEARL HARBOR ATTACK.

out onto the roof and looked northwest toward Pearl Harbor. Black pillars of smoke billowed high into the sky.

He raced back to the radio in time to hear another urgent bulletin. All cadets in the Reserve Officers' Training Corps (ROTC)—the college program that prepared students to join the military—were to report to the University of Hawai'i gym immediately. That meant him. Kats threw on his uniform and sprinted to the campus, joining a stream of young men rushing toward the gym.

Inside the building, five hundred cadets were milling around in noisy confusion. Someone had dragged in crates of old rifles, and the men started cleaning the guns and trying to figure out how to put in the firing pins. Their training hadn't yet covered handling weapons.

From time to time, they heard aircraft roaring overhead. None of the young men sitting anxiously on the hardwood floor of the gym clutching their guns knew what to expect next or what was happening outside. Then word spread that an invasion had begun and that Japanese paratroopers were landing on the hills right above campus.

They all rushed out and peered up the hill. Sure enough, they could make out figures moving through the kiawe trees up on the heights. Someone ordered the stunned young men to prepare to repel an enemy assault.

Kats stood staring up the hill, clutching his rifle, aghast. That morning, he had been planning his trip home for Christmas, and now all hell had broken loose.

★ ★ ★ ★

Home for Kats was the small hotel his family ran in the port town of Kahului on the island of Maui. Small and rickety as it was, the Miho Hotel was nevertheless a happy and vibrant home, where guests and family alike enjoyed Japanese dinners, soaked in a large ofuro hot tub, fell asleep to the sound of palm fronds rustling in the trade winds, and woke in the morning to the shrill whistles of the steam locomotives that pulled the sugar trains through town.

THE MIHO KIDS ON MAUI (LEFT TO RIGHT): PAUL, KATS, FUMIYE, KATSUAKI. KATS MIHO AT MAUI HIGH.

At the center of the hotel was a lush courtyard where Kats's mother, Ayano, grew orchids and other tropical flowers—sweet explosions of pink, lavender, and red set among dark green foliage. Kats's father, Katsuichi, was a thin and dapper man with an impeccably trimmed mustache. A school principal in Japan, he'd become a businessman only by necessity after immigrating to Hawai'i. Maui's large Japanese community held him in high esteem, and he spent most of his time bustling around town, tending to community affairs. He distributed a Japanese-language newspaper, cultivated Japanese culture, kept the old ways alive. That was important to him.

★ ★ ★ ★

The city of Honolulu was gripped by terror that night. Even though the "Japanese paratroopers" in the hills turned out to be hikers, trying to get a better look at Pearl Harbor, everyone still expected a Japanese invasion. Young men like Kats were stationed along the waterfront, every fifty yards or so. Everyone was jittery, trigger-happy.

Kats stood peering into the dark, armed only with an ancient rifle he didn't know how to use and five rounds of ammunition. From time to time, he was startled by an unexpected sound—the sudden bark of a dog, someone dropping something into a trash can, a door slamming. But despite everything, he felt proud. After a long day feeling angry and helpless, he was in uniform, armed, and serving his country, protecting it from those who would do it harm.

Earlier that day, Kats and his fellow ROTC cadets—virtually all Americans of Japanese ancestry—were transferred into an entirely new entity, the Hawai'i Territorial Guard. Their mission was to guard O'ahu's infrastructure—power plants, pumping stations, fuel depots—against the expected Japanese invasion.

Wild rumors spread through the darkened city. That Japanese nationals living in Hawai'i had poisoned the water supply. That Japanese plantation workers had cut large arrows in the cane fields to direct enemy planes. That Japanese troops had come ashore. That Japanese Americans armed with machine guns had opened fire on the air force base Hickam Field. None of them turned out to be true.

What Kats didn't know was that while he stood guard with his gun in Honolulu, over on Maui, other men with guns— FBI agents—were taking his father away. Katsuichi, believing he was about to be executed, turned to Ayano, weeping in the doorway of the hotel, and told her, "Don't do anything that will bring shame to the family and the Japanese race. Do your best no matter what. Keep your self-dignity."[5]

Katsuichi was just one of hundreds of mostly older Japanese men taken from their homes that evening and one of thousands arrested both in Hawai'i and on the US mainland over the next several weeks. Almost all were Issei—immigrants to the United States. Most of them had lived in the United States for decades, although by law they were not allowed to become citizens.

Their American-born children—known as Nisei— were American citizens and therefore protected by the US Constitution from unwarranted arrest. That protection would soon turn out to be an illusion.

In Honolulu, a bank building was used to process the Issei men as they were brought in. One man, a temple priest so bent by age he could hardly walk, was escorted by a young Japanese American soldier. The soldier stared glumly at the ground, mortified by what he was being required to do. Some of the men being questioned spoke little English and simply did not understand what was happening to them. One asked his son and daughter-in-law, "What means Jap?"[6]

CHAPTER 2

—✗——✗——✗——✗——✗——✗——✗—

THERE WERE FORTY-FIVE MILLION RADIOS in the United States in 1941, and on any given Sunday morning most of them were likely to be turned on. That was when life offered working Americans an opportunity to sit down and pick up knitting needles, or a newspaper, or a panful of peas in need of shelling and enjoy a broadcast.

One of the radios turned on that day was in an apartment over a small commercial laundry in the Hillyard neighborhood of Spokane, Washington. The owners of the Hillyard Laundry, Kisaburo and Tori Shiosaki, were relaxing after another long week's work. It was a cold day—not quite freezing, but just on the edge of it. The apartment was cozy and warm, with the wet heat rising from the big laundry boilers downstairs steaming up the windows, and it was full of comfortable Sunday morning smells: eggs frying, toast browning, tea brewing on the stove. Tori was thinking that she might go downtown to the Methodist church to visit with some of the Japanese ladies there. After a week struggling

TORI AND KISABURO SHIOSAKI AT WORK IN THE HILLYARD LAUNDRY.

to communicate with her customers in English, she enjoyed being able to speak Japanese.

It was Fred, her seventeen-year-old son, who had turned the radio on. He was listening to *The World Today*, a CBS news show, when, at 11:30 a.m., an agitated voice interrupted the broadcast: "The Japanese have attacked Pearl Harbor, Hawai'i, by air, President Roosevelt has just announced."

Startled, Fred called to his father in the next room. "Hey, Pop! The Japanese have attacked Hawai'i!"[7]

Fred's parents and his siblings gathered around the radio. His parents looked pale and tense. Fred sat stunned, as hateful words poured out of the radio, sounding more and more venomous each time.

"The Japs."

"The dirty Japs."

"The dirty yellow Japs."

This time, the word "Jap" wasn't coming from where Fred usually heard it—out of the mouths of teenage bullies at school or on the streets of Hillyard. It was coming from adults, from news announcers, military officials, figures of respect and authority. It seemed to be coming from the heart of America itself.

For Fred's parents, the word, and the tone, came as no surprise. Since arriving in America, they had been mistreated often enough, had heard the word hurled at them often enough, to know that as friendly as their customers might be, much of the country had long since hardened its heart against people who looked like them.

In the first few hours, Americans' reactions ran the gamut from rage to fear to relief. Many young men, particularly those already in uniform, saw their futures as suddenly more interesting, with the possibility of glory awaiting them in a war that was now just over the western horizon. A soldier on leave in Atlanta crowed, "Oh boy, this is it!" Another, in Portland, Oregon, turned to a friend, smiled, and said, "We'd better polish up our shootin' irons."

Most Americans were, unsurprisingly, just plain angry—and raring to do something about it. In St. Louis, Missouri, Sunday worshippers agreed that "they ought to blow the Japanese navy out of the water."[8] In Kansas City, a newsboy yelled, "Gotta whip those Japs!"[9] His customers nodded, handed him coins, and took their papers.

On Monday morning, Fred stayed home from school and remained indoors all day. He was deeply anxious, his stomach in a knot. He knew he could scrap with the best, one-on-one, but he was one of only a few Japanese American students at his high school, and he wasn't at all sure the whole school wouldn't jump him the moment he walked into the building.

At the laundry, the day did not go well. His parents opened at the usual time—7:00 a.m.—but by midmorning no customers had come in. Kisaburo drove over to the home of Will Simpson—the editor of the *Hillyard News* and a long-time friend—to pick up Simpson's laundry, as he did every Monday morning.

For more than twenty years, Simpson had been Kisaburo's mentor and an important ally. Now when Kisaburo appeared at his back door, Simpson held up the front page of the Spokane *Spokesman-Review*, containing the first horrifying casualty figures from Hawai'i. "What do you think of that?" Simpson demanded.

Kisaburo didn't know what to say. Finally, he murmured, "It was dumb of them. I'm sure it will be over soon." Simpson stared at him, hard, as if he were seeing him for the first time, and said, "Well, I'm afraid I can't do business with you anymore. I have a political position I have to be careful of." With that, he shut the door in Kisaburo's face.

When he returned to the laundry, Kisaburo found his family waiting, hoping he would have work, something for them to do. But Fred could see at a glance that his father was empty-handed and utterly crestfallen. Kisaburo muttered, "Mr. Simpson said . . . well, he's not going to do business with us anymore."[10]

He sat quietly behind the counter for the rest of the morning, thinking about the apparent ruin of everything he had worked so hard to achieve over three decades in the United States. Fred had never seen him so crushed.

Kisaburo had come to America with a wicker suitcase and a head full of dreams. As the third son of a tenant farmer, he had no prospects at all in Japan—nothing beyond a life of labor and extreme poverty. When recruiters came to his village seeking workers for the Canadian Pacific Railway, he lunged at the opportunity and boarded a steamer to Vancouver.

The railroad work was desperately hard and paid low wages—just a dollar or two a day. Kisaburo and his fellow Japanese immigrants endured the long Canadian winters, wielding picks and shovels with frozen hands in relentless sleet and snow. At night, they slept in boxcars or tents and huddled around campfires, cooking rice and bits of fish and whatever else they could afford on their meager wages.

In the summers, they toiled under a broiling sun. Many of them suffered from scurvy, a disease caused by a lack of fresh fruit and vegetables. Some were maimed in explosions or crushed under tons of falling rock. It was a miserable existence, with mere survival the best a man could hope for.

When the section of railway track Kisaburo was working on brought him close to the US border, he decided he'd had enough and slipped across into the United States. He worked his way toward Washington State, where he found a job at the elegant Davenport Hotel in Spokane.

For the young man who had grown up in poverty in rural Japan, simply walking into the luxurious lobby of the hotel was entering another world. But the work was anything but elegant. Men his own age called him "boy." He cleared tables, toted stacks of greasy plates into the kitchen, emptied spittoons and ashtrays, mopped restrooms, scrubbed dishes—anything that was asked of him—for nine or ten hours a day, six days a week.

Nevertheless, compared to years toiling on the railroad, it was nothing to Kisaburo. He poured his heart into every task. Within a year, he had so impressed his employers that they wrote him a glowing letter of recommendation, and with that in hand—and wearing a new suit and carrying a silk umbrella as evidence of his prosperity—he sailed for Japan to find a wife.

Tori Iwai lived in the village of Hatsuma, within walking distance of Kisaburo's home village. The two were promptly married with the blessings of both sets of parents. Kisaburo returned to Spokane and bought the laundry, and Tori followed soon after. They leaped into their suddenly bright future together, working long hours, making friends in the community, and building a family.

By early 1941, they were secure. They were not the kind of people who could stay at the Davenport, or even have a meal there. Sometimes signs outside businesses informed them that they and their children were not welcome. Certain neighborhoods prevented them from buying a home, even if they had the money to do so. Random strangers sneered at them and called them "Japs." But they had a thriving business, a home, an automobile, and children who were getting educations that would almost certainly allow them to rise into the American middle class.

That was before Pearl Harbor.

Fred returned reluctantly to school. His mother insisted. When he arrived at John R. Rogers High, his heart was racing and his stomach was churning. He took a deep breath, pushed his way through one of the four massive front doors, and made his way into the school's clamoring hallways.

Students were huddled in clusters, talking excitedly about the war. They seemed too absorbed by the casualty figures and the prospect that the young men among them would soon all be in uniform to take any particular note of Fred. If anything, people seemed to avert their eyes.

By midmorning, to his enormous relief, he found that his friends were still his friends. His buddies on the track team still wanted to talk about the upcoming season. His friends in the photography club were already making assignments for next June's yearbook. But those were his friends. And that was just the first few hours.

As the day wore on, Fred realized that while nobody was going to assault him at school, he now stood apart from most of the student body. Conversations dissolved into silence when he attempted to join in. Friendly glances were returned with blank stares. Backs were suddenly turned when he approached. And every afternoon he returned home to find the laundry machinery quiet and his parents idle and despondent.

CHAPTER 3

—✕——✕——✕——✕——✕——✕——✕—

IN JAPAN, KATS MIHO'S SISTER, Fumiye, was teaching English in her classroom in suburban Tokyo when a young Russian teacher named Miss Zabriaski burst in. "Miss Miho, Miss Miho! War between Japan, America!"

Fumiye smiled and laughed her off. "No, no, that's just propaganda,"[11] she said, and went on teaching. Miss Zabriaski looked exasperated, muttered something in Russian, and ran from the room.

Fed up with the racial discrimination she experienced growing up in Hawai'i, Fumiye had come to Japan in the spring of 1940, shortly after graduating from the University of Hawai'i. A famous scholar, Dr. Junjiro Takakusu, saw Fumiye's academic potential and suggested she enroll for graduate studies at Japan's most prestigious university, Tokyo Imperial.

Fumiye set sail for Japan almost without a second thought. It was only after she arrived that she discovered Dr. Takakusu had overlooked one crucial detail: women were not allowed to enroll at Tokyo Imperial. Nevertheless, she decided to stay in Japan and moved in with her older sister, Tsukie, and Tsukie's husband, a dentist.

With great enthusiasm, Fumiye threw herself into her new life. She found jobs teaching English part-time. She took lessons in ikebana—the Japanese art of flower arranging—and dressed in a kimono for the tea ceremony every Friday. She developed a deep interest in Kabuki theater.

For the first time in her life, she felt that she was fully a part of the society in which she lived, as if she truly belonged. She knew that she would not be judged by her appearance or held back by her race.

Sure, tensions between the country where she had been born and the country where she chose to live were on the rise, but no matter. There were many good, kind people in both countries. So that morning, when Miss Zabriaski rushed into her classroom shouting about war, Fumiye immediately put it out of her mind and focused on her students.

Walking home that afternoon, she realized that something was, in fact, going on. Then, on a newsstand, she saw a shocking headline: entire US Navy destroyed in Hawai'i. She ran the rest of the way home, burst into the house, and fell sobbing into her sister's arms. The two women tried to comfort each other, wondering aloud and fearing silently what might be happening to their family in Hawai'i.

★ ★ ★ ★

When the FBI came for him at the Miho Hotel, Katsuichi Miho had been frightened but not really surprised. He knew that his dedication to keeping Japanese culture alive in Hawai'i was likely to look suspicious to the American authorities.

He was taken to Sand Island, a bleak expanse of sand and dead coral in Honolulu Harbor, where soldiers herded him and roughly 450 other Issei men into a five-acre enclosure surrounded by a barbed-wire fence. Eight towers, guarded by soldiers with machine guns, stood at intervals around the perimeter. The Issei men were assigned canvas tents, each with eight cots laid directly on the mud and coral.

AGENTS ARRESTING ISSEI MEN.

It rained for days on end that December, and the tents flooded. Several times a day, the men had to stand outside, in the driving rain, for roll call. They shivered in their wet clothes day and night. They had no access to phones, radios, newspapers, pens, paper, wristwatches, or even bars of soap. The guards referred to them as prisoners of war. They had little idea about what was happening in the outside world and no idea at all about what was going to happen to them.

For those outside the camp, with access to radios and newspapers, the war news just kept getting worse. Japanese imperial forces seized Hong Kong, invaded Thailand, and bombed Guam and the Philippines. On December 12 they landed troops in the Philippines, and on December 14 they invaded Burma.

They even returned to Hawai'i. At dusk on December 15, a Japanese submarine surfaced off Maui and lobbed ten shells into Kahului, damaging a pineapple cannery. Only two chickens died in the attack, but it had its desired effect, terrorizing the town's inhabitants and reinforcing the belief that a Japanese invasion of Hawai'i was imminent.

As the bad news continued to roll in, the nation's angriest voices became the loudest, unleashing a torrent of racist invective that all but drowned out those still able to take a step back and distinguish between friend and foe.

Politicians who knew how to use racial hatred to their advantage seized the opportunity, and their rhetoric quickly became brazenly toxic. Representative John Rankin of Mississippi declared, "This is a race war . . . I say it is of vital importance that we get rid of every Japanese . . . Let's get rid of them now!"[12]

Since the earliest days of Asian immigration in the nineteenth century, certain US newspapers warned about what they called the "Yellow Peril," claiming that the arrival of too many people from Asia would engulf white American civilization and culture.

In the 1920s, Hollywood reinforced this notion, giving the world the character of Fu Manchu, an evil criminal mastermind hell-bent on destroying the Western world. Other unsavory Asian characters—almost always played by white actors—were common in American movies. By the 1940s, the racist caricatures and the hatred they roused were ingrained in the minds of millions of Americans.

Now, in the aftermath of Pearl Harbor, Japanese American children were taunted on their way to school, barred from public amusement parks, turned away from theaters. Restaurants and hair salons, pharmacies, and dental offices refused to serve Japanese American customers. People boycotted Japanese businesses. The president of the University of Arizona forbade the library to lend books to Japanese American students, declaring that "these people are our enemies."[13]

★★★★

For nearly six weeks, Kats Miho and his fellow guardsmen of the Hawai'i Territorial Guard patrolled O'ahu. From the first moment they heard the news of Pearl Harbor—or witnessed the attack with their own eyes—they knew they would bear a particular burden in this war. More than three-quarters of their number were Japanese American, and their faces and last names suggested a connection with the enemy. They were determined to prove that they were just as American—and just as eager to fight—as anyone else.

Then, early on January 19, came a blow they never expected. Kats and his squad were picked up from their post and brought to an athletics field, where they found the entire Territorial Guard milling around in the predawn dark, wondering why they were there. Finally, one of their commanding officers explained—tears welling in his eyes as he spoke.

Captain Nolle Smith was a large man, a halfback on the University of Hawai'i football team. As a Black man, he knew something about discrimination. He said that he had tried to stop what was about to happen, that all the local officers had tried, but that they were overruled by someone in Washington, DC.

Then, another officer took over and got bluntly to the heart of the matter. Some of the brass visiting from the mainland had been upset to see men who appeared to be Japanese carrying guns. Orders had come down. "The reason you are here is because you—all you Americans of Japanese ancestry—because of your ethnic background, you are being discharged from the Hawaiian Territorial Guard."[14]

Kats stood stunned, his mouth open. They were all

stunned. And angry. And humiliated. All they had wanted since the morning of December 7 was to serve their country. Now that opportunity had been taken away, replaced with the realization that they—Japanese Americans—were not trusted. Worse even than that, they were not seen as truly American.

For a few moments, there was only silence. Then Kats heard men weeping softly in the darkness all around him.

CHAPTER 4

————✕——✕——✕——✕——✕——✕——✕————

SPRING CAME EARLY IN 1942, as it often does in California's Salinas Valley, where vast fields of lettuce, chard, spinach, and artichokes stretch from the Gabilán mountains in the east all the way to the great blue crescent of Monterey Bay in the west. Less than a century after Americans from eastern states swept into California in search of gold, displacing the original Mexican families from the valley's sprawling ranchos, white Americans now owned most of the land.

But it was mainly Chinese, Filipino, and Japanese immigrants who worked that land. It was they who grew, harvested, and shipped east the bulk of the nation's fresh green produce, they whose labor had, by the 1930s, turned the valley into "America's Salad Bowl."

The work was tough, unrelenting, and poorly paid, and so were many of the kids who grew up in the valley. Few were tougher than sixteen-year-old Rudy Tokiwa. Slight of build, born prematurely, and asthmatic, Rudy had always been a fighter.

On the day of the Pearl Harbor attack, he was standing in a field of lettuce, leaning on a hoe. His sister, Fumi, brought him the news, running across the field toward him, waving her arms and yelling.

Rudy had been alarmed but not really surprised. His first thought was *Well, it had to happen.* Then, almost immediately, a second thought—a question—came to mind. If this meant war, war with Japan, what would he do if called upon to fight?

For Rudy, that was a complex question. Like many young Japanese Americans, Rudy had spent time in Japan—living with family members, learning the language, and getting to know his parents' culture. As a schoolboy in his family's ancestral prefecture, Kagoshima in southern Japan, he found Japanese life to be far harder and harsher than he had expected.

When he was thirteen, he and his classmates had to do military training. They could be summoned by bugle from their beds at any hour of the night and sent out on military exercises in the countryside. Sometimes the maneuvers went on for forty-eight hours straight, with the teenagers stumbling across fields, staggering under the weight of heavy packs. If Rudy hadn't remembered to have food ready to bring with him, he went hungry.

Rudy also witnessed firsthand how hard everyday life was in Japan. A US oil embargo, designed to punish Japanese

RUDY TOKIWA.

aggression in China, meant that buses, cars, and taxis ran on coal rather than on gasoline. As a result, the air was polluted and sooty. Consumer goods were scarce, and necessities like rice were rationed.

The national mood darkened under the strain of the oil embargo, and it seemed that war against America was inevitable. By the fall of 1939, Rudy's Japanese uncle decided it would be prudent to send his nephew home.

Without much difficulty, Rudy stepped back into the all-American life he had known before his time abroad. He and his mostly white friends from school hung out at soda fountains, went to the movies, tinkered with cars. Lean, lithe, and hardened by his experiences in Japan, he took up gymnastics, track, and wrestling. Lightly built as he was, he nevertheless joined the Salinas Cowboys, his high school's football team.

But Rudy's outlook on life was not the same as it had been before he left for Japan. He felt that he had become a better young man there: tougher, better able to cope with adversity, more aware of the virtues of hard work and discipline. He came home deeply proud of his Japanese heritage and conscious of how isolated and besieged the Japanese felt on the world stage.

He knew—far better than most Americans—just how close war was, how inevitable it seemed from the Japanese point of view. And so he was not surprised when his sister caught up with him in the lettuce field on December 7 and told him the news.

That evening, the Tokiwa family did what thousands of Japanese families across America were doing. They gathered up family photographs and Japanese dolls and works of Japanese literature and threw them on the fire. They smashed Japanese gramophone records. They took apart Buddhist and Shinto shrines. They gave away—to astonished neighbors—lovely kimonos, antique vases, and heirloom samurai swords. They discarded anything made in Japan—cameras, binoculars, dinnerware. Rudy's father, Jisuke—a US Army veteran from World War I—carefully laid his service uniform on top of a pile of clothes in an old steamer trunk, to be sure that anyone opening the trunk would see it first.

The next morning, as Rudy and his brother, Duke, were walking to school, half a dozen boys stepped in front of them, jabbed fingers in their chests, and snarled, "Them dirty Japs. Let's beat them up." Rudy and Duke exchanged glances. Then Duke growled, "Aw, we can handle them." The brothers cocked their fists, but before they could engage, a voice behind them shouted, "All right, you Tokiwa brothers, step aside. We'll handle it." It was a good portion of the Salinas Cowboys football team. The bullies took off running.[15]

But when Rudy and Duke entered the school building and walked down the halls, more kids began jeering at them: "There go them Japs." Rudy stormed into the principal's office and said that he and his brother were going home. The principal let them go, but not before making it clear he thought Rudy was a troublemaker.

There was more trouble at home. FBI agents broke down the front door and ransacked the house, pulling out drawers and dumping their contents on the floor, rummaging through closets, climbing into the attic to search for shortwave radios, binoculars, cameras—anything that might be useful to saboteurs or spies or suggest loyalty to the Empire of Japan.

When one found Jisuke's World War I uniform, he held it up and asked, "What's this?"

"That's my uniform," Jisuke replied quietly.

"This is an American uniform."

"Well, I was in the American army. I went to France."

"Aw, the American army never took no Japs." The agent threw the uniform on the floor and trampled it underfoot.

That was too much for Rudy. He leaped to his feet and screamed, "Go to hell! Go to hell!"[16] His parents restrained him, but Rudy stood seething until the agents had gone.

Now, eight weeks after Pearl Harbor, Rudy was even angrier. First, his parents had been told they couldn't travel more than twelve miles from home without permission, which meant they couldn't get into downtown Salinas to buy things they needed—groceries and household goods and farm supplies. Then, when his sister, Fumi, had gone to a nearby farm store to buy seed, she'd been quietly told to come back later when there weren't any white customers in the store to see the transaction.

And rumors were circulating. Word was that thousands of Japanese American families might soon be forced out of their homes and locked up like criminals. That wasn't likely, thought Rudy. Not whole families. After all, second-generation Americans of Japanese descent—Nisei like himself—were citizens of the United States. At Salinas High he'd learned about the Constitution. American citizens had rights. They couldn't just lock them up for nothing. But what, he wondered, would become of his parents?

CHAPTER 5

IN SPOKANE, FRED SHIOSAKI AND his family lived in fear that at any moment FBI agents might come and take Fred's father, Kisaburo, away. One by one the other Issei men in the town had been arrested, and their families had not heard from them since.

When the FBI did show up, they ordered Fred's parents to report to their office. Fred and his sister, Blanche, drove their parents downtown and waited outside in the car. Hours ticked by, and the siblings worried that their father would vanish, as other fathers had vanished. Finally their parents emerged from the building. Kisaburo and Tori got into the car and announced quietly that they were now something called "enemy aliens."

Barely a week after Pearl Harbor, Congressman John Rankin of Mississippi strode onto the floor of the House of Representatives and declared, "I'm for catching every Japanese in America, Alaska, and Hawaii now and putting them in concentration camps."[17] Some in the Roosevelt administration pushed back, citing a lack of evidence and concerns over what the law allowed.

The War Department and military commanders also pushed for mass incarcerations. The Department of Justice argued against, saying that this would be a massive violation of civil rights. Throughout late January and early February, the two sides debated the issue in a series of contentious meetings.

All the while, pressure mounted on President Franklin D. Roosevelt, from military officials, West Coast journalists, and both Democratic and Republican politicians. They wanted those people removed. Now. Increasingly, Roosevelt seemed inclined to agree with them.

Eleanor Roosevelt did not. Immediately after Pearl Harbor, the first lady had made a point of posing for photographs with a group of Nisei, and she made a radio address on January 11 in which she pointed out that the Issei were long-term residents who had always been denied the right to apply for citizenship.

Back at the White House, she tried to gain the president's ear, but to no avail. On February 19, 1942, President Roosevelt signed Executive Order 9066, authorizing the secretary of war, or his military commanders, to designate areas of the country from which "any and all persons may be excluded."

The order made no mention of Japanese Americans, nor

of any other ethnic group. It made no distinction between citizens and noncitizens. It did not specify what was to become of whoever was excluded, where they were to be sent, or what was to be done with them. All that was left to the military authorities.

But everyone knew at whom the order was aimed: anyone and everyone with a Japanese surname living near the West Coast of the United States. The western sections of Washington State, Oregon, and California and parts of Arizona were designated an "exclusion zone" from which both Japanese Americans and their Issei parents were to move or be removed. The majority of America's Issei and Nisei lived within these boundaries.

The only other large concentration of Japanese Americans—and it was very large—was in Hawai'i. The government realized it would be impossible to lock up so many people without devastating the sugar and pineapple industries. That could not be allowed to happen.

In Hawai'i, only those the FBI considered overly friendly to Japan would be incarcerated. They would be kept in federal detention sites, mostly on the mainland, far away from their families. And so, on the morning of March 17, Katsuichi Miho and 165 other Issei men were marched into the hold of an old steamship and taken to the mainland.

They were brought first to San Francisco, then to Fort Sill in Oklahoma, just north of the Texas border. The place was nearly treeless—a windy, flat landscape unlike anything they had ever seen. Accommodation was in four-man canvas tents, and the camp was surrounded by two fences, the outer one topped with rolls of barbed wire. Overlooking the stockade stood a guard tower with searchlights and a machine gun.

A day or two after their arrival, each of the Issei men was called in turn into a makeshift clinic and told to strip. Expecting to be vaccinated, Katsuichi waited patiently for a doctor. Instead, someone who was not a doctor came into the room and slowly and deliberately wrote a number across his bare chest with a red pen. This number was now his identity as far as the government was concerned.

At night, Katsuichi lay on his cot in the dark, staring at the canvas above his head as the searchlight played over the tents. Listening to the wind whistle and his tentmates snore, he tried to conjure up the Miho Hotel: the pink and white orchids Ayano grew in the courtyard, the smell of ginger and shoyu drifting from the kitchen, the soothing warm water of his wood-heated ofuro, the laughter of his children.

But try as he might, he couldn't hold on to the images. They seemed far out of reach, rapidly disappearing into the past.

★★★★

A new government agency, the War Relocation Authority (WRA), was established by President Roosevelt on March 18. Its purpose was to incarcerate people who had been removed from California and parts of Washington State, Oregon, and Arizona.

A week later, on March 24, the army issued the first of a series of area-specific civilian "evacuation" orders. This first order applied to 271 people of Japanese ancestry living on Bainbridge Island in Washington State. It gave them six days to prepare to be taken away to camps the government called "assembly centers," and they were allowed to take only what they could carry.

A FAMILY BEING FORCIBLY REMOVED FROM BAINBRIDGE ISLAND.

To be sure, there were families who stepped forward to help their Japanese American friends, neighbors, and business associates. But others couldn't wait to see them go. They wanted to take over the leases on their homes and farmland, buy out their businesses for a fraction of their worth, loot their possessions, and vandalize their orchards and greenhouses.

Men in trucks drove around Bainbridge Island, looking to take advantage. "Hey, you Japs! I'll give you ten bucks for that refrigerator . . . I'll give you two bucks and fifty cents for that washing machine."[18]

★ ★ ★ ★

In Salinas, Rudy's father was at a loss. Headlines in newspapers, posters plastered on telephone poles, and stern bulletins on the radio were all telling him that by April 30 he and his family would be required to "evacuate"—to walk away from the land, leaving his crops to wither and die in the ground. It seemed more than a man his age should have to bear.

In the forty-two years since Jisuke Tokiwa left Japan, he had been a houseboy, a student, a laborer, an American soldier, and a farmer. After a life of hard work, he had allowed himself to believe that he and his wife, Fusa, would be reasonably comfortable in their old age, that they could begin to enjoy life a little and let their sons carry more of the weight of running the farm.

Now those dreams lay shattered.

The Tokiwas did not own the land they farmed—Japanese immigrants were banned from owning land by anti-Asian laws reaching back to the arrival of Chinese laborers during the gold rush of 1849. Nor were they allowed to become American citizens. Now they faced forced removal from their homes, loss of their livelihoods, and mass incarceration.

The Tokiwas' neighbors, Ed and Henry Pozzi, were immigrants themselves, from an Italian Swiss family. Years before, when the Pozzi boys were orphaned, Jisuke had advised them to switch from dairy production to crops, with enormous success, and he had mentored them on everything from tractor maintenance to seed selection.

Now that the Tokiwas were in a difficult situation, the brothers were eager to help.

"You store everything in our place," Ed and Henry said.[19]

"Are you sure you want to do that? You might get in trouble."

"No, no, you people are like family to us." They even agreed to take care of Fumi's dog.

On April 30, 1942, Rudy's father turned the key in his front door, and the Pozzi brothers drove the family downtown, where they joined hundreds of people milling around on the sidewalk.

Many had come dressed in their Sunday best—men in three-piece suits, ties, and fedoras; women wearing white gloves, pumps, and church hats; little girls in plaid skirts and black patent-leather shoes. They came carrying bags and suitcases, dragging steamer trunks, and cradling babies and jewelry boxes.

FAMILIES WITH PERSONAL POSSESSIONS STACKED
IN FRONT OF THE SALINAS ARMORY.

A YOUNG GIRL IN OAKLAND, CALIFORNIA, TAGGED AND READY TO BE
SENT TO AN "ASSEMBLY CENTER."

The Tokiwas piled their possessions on the growing mountain of luggage, where men in military uniforms attached paper tags to the bundles. Then they attached matching tags to Rudy, his parents, and his siblings.

More uniformed men directed them into a crowded auditorium, where they sat on folding chairs waiting to register. Eventually their names were called. They filled out some forms, then trooped back outside and climbed reluctantly onto a Greyhound bus. A grim silence settled over the passengers as the reality of what was happening sank in.

It was a short ride, just across town, to the Salinas Rodeo Grounds. When he got off the bus, Rudy was shocked. He tried to imagine it in advance, to prepare himself for it, but the sight of the barbed-wire fencing and the rows of barracks made of tar paper and pine planks drove home the reality of his future and deepened his outrage at the injustice.

The Tokiwas found their belongings and dragged them through the dust, past a row of tall eucalyptus trees and a barbed-wire gate, into what was now called the Salinas Assembly Center. It was a concentration camp.

They found their assigned barracks and peered into the single room they were all to occupy. There was no furniture apart from some metal cots, a couple of light bulbs hanging from the ceiling, and a kerosene stove in the middle of the room. A plywood partition between their room and the next did not even reach the ceiling, and they could hear every word spoken by the family next door.

Over the next few days, Rudy explored the camp. It was basic and poorly equipped. The men's toilets were nothing more than planks with holes in them placed over pits in the ground. There was a long line to use them, and they stank. There was no privacy. In the men's bathhouses, shower faucets had been placed seven feet up on the walls—too high for many boys and some adults to reach.

When he went to the mess hall to find something to eat, Rudy discovered that it, too, required standing in line— sometimes for forty-five minutes. The food was sparse at best. With a food budget of just thirty-three cents per day for each person in the camp, there was usually rice or potatoes but seldom any meat—a bit of tongue or liver at most.

BARRACKS AT CAMP HARMONY AT THE PUYALLUP FAIRGROUNDS.

The worst of it, for Rudy as for most people, was the barbed wire around the camp and the watchtowers guarded by uniformed men armed with guns.

Conditions were much the same at the fourteen other hastily built assembly centers—what newspapers around the country had taken to calling "Jap Camps"[20]—in Washington State, Oregon, California, and Arizona.

At the Puyallup Fairgrounds, south of Seattle, where the assembly center was almost insultingly called Camp Harmony, rain turned the ground into soupy mud, and people sank to their ankles every time they stepped outside. At the Santa Anita racetrack in Arcadia, California, dozens of families were housed in horse stalls that reeked of manure and urine. For young Americans like Rudy, who had grown up free and proudly American, and for their entire families, it was all deeply humiliating and starkly dehumanizing.

CHAPTER 6

— ✖ — ✖ — ✖ — ✖ — ✖ — ✖ — ✖ —

GORDON HIRABAYASHI WAS HALFWAY ACROSS campus when it hit him.

He was in a hurry, on his way home to his dingy basement room in the YMCA, across the street from the University of Washington in Seattle. A few minutes before, he'd been in the library, studying with some of his classmates. They reminded him about the curfew that had been imposed on all people of Japanese ancestry—citizens and noncitizens alike. From 8:00 p.m. until 6:00 a.m., they were not allowed outside their homes. He would need to hurry, his classmates said.

Gordon said his goodbyes and left the library, walking briskly. Then, suddenly, he stopped dead in his tracks, realizing for the first time the unfairness of what he was being required to do.

Why did *he* have to be home by 8:00 p.m. when none of his classmates did? On what basis, other than race, was there a distinction between him and them? And if the only difference was race, how could that be consistent with the Constitution he had studied in high school?

So Gordon turned around and headed back to the library. His classmates, startled to see him reappear, said, "Hey! What are you doing here?"

"I'll go back when you guys are ready to go."

And with that he sat down, opened his books, and resumed studying.[21]

Gordon Hirabayashi was one of those people who are determined to find their own path through life. He was a resolute and unflappable young man. He chose his words carefully, deploying them deliberately in a slow, measured way that invited close attention to each and every one. He had grown up in the White River valley, south of Seattle, where his parents grew vegetables and raised their son to follow his own moral compass, defend just principles, and align his actions with his beliefs. Gordon wanted to live a courageous life, and the essence of courage, as he saw it, was holding fast to fundamental truths, regardless of how inconvenient or painful the consequences.

When he first entered the University of Washington, Gordon enrolled in the ROTC program, but after participating in a debate about the military draft he moved toward pacifism and nonviolence. By 1940, well before Pearl Harbor, he left the ROTC and registered with the Selective Service (the government agency responsible for administering the draft) as a conscientious objector.

As the deadline for the forced removal of Japanese Americans from Seattle approached, Gordon dropped out of the university and went to work for the local Quaker chapter, helping the families of Issei men who had been imprisoned by the Department of Justice. With their husbands and fathers gone, many women and children needed help preparing for their own incarceration—selling their possessions, closing businesses, packing, figuring out how much they could carry to the buses that were to take them to the camps.

Gordon soon realized that old women and men with canes couldn't carry much of anything. Mothers carrying infants couldn't also manage a cradle or diapers or extra clothing for the baby. Furniture, automobiles, and cherished heirlooms couldn't be carried at all and so had to be given away, sold for pennies on the dollar, or stored for who knew how long at who knew what cost.

And personal possessions were the least of it. Anxiety, depression, and fear stalked Japanese American communities up and down the West Coast. Gordon volunteered to help as parents sat children down and explained they would have to give up beloved pets. He counseled students who realized they would have to quit classes midsemester, say goodbye to their closest friends, miss senior proms, perhaps even forgo diplomas they had all but earned. He found experts to advise anxious business owners forced to close businesses they had nurtured for decades.

As the date approached on which Gordon himself was required to register, he decided that he wouldn't do it. He couldn't. Not if he were to remain true to his principles. As an American, he simply could not surrender his constitutional rights as if they meant nothing, as if they were mere words scrawled on an old piece of parchment.

Once he had made up his mind, Gordon's main concern was that he didn't get his Quaker associates or his friends at the YMCA in trouble for harboring a fugitive. He wanted to make it clear that he alone was responsible for what he was about to do.

He told a few select friends what he planned. Then he phoned his parents to explain his decision. It was a hard conversation because they expected him to join them on their bus. His mother began to cry. She hadn't expected them to have to part ways. She agreed with him in principle, respected his position, and admired him for his courage, but she was desperately afraid for him.

"Please put your principles aside on this occasion," she pleaded. "Come home and move with us. Heaven knows what will become of you if you confront the government."

"I'd like to," Gordon said, "but I wouldn't be the same person if I went now."

As he put down the phone receiver, Gordon was crying, too. But he would not budge. Not even for his mother. And so, when the last bus to Camp Harmony pulled out of town on May 12, Gordon was not on it.

He was now the last Japanese American living in Seattle. The next day, he sat down at a typewriter and pecked out a statement addressed to the FBI. He handed copies to officials at the YMCA, the director of the ROTC program, and several of his Quaker friends.

Later that week, he went with his lawyer to the FBI offices in the Vance Building at Third and Union in Seattle. Special Agent Francis Manion glanced at Gordon's statement and said, "Oh, we already have that. We've been expecting you."

Gordon wanted it made clear that he was surrendering voluntarily, not because someone had intercepted his statement or turned him in. "Here is the original," he said. "I'd like to leave it with you."

"Okay," Manion said. "We'll take it."

Now that they had him, the FBI couldn't figure out what to do with Gordon. They drove him over to where Japanese Americans were supposed to register, and someone put a paper in front of him.

"That looks like the same registration form I saw a few days ago," Gordon said. "Has there been any change in it?"

"Well, no."

"Then I can't sign it."

"But you have to sign it. Everyone has to sign it," Manion said.

Gordon, unruffled, asked, "Have you signed it?"

Taken aback, Manion replied, "If you don't sign it, you are breaking the law, and you're subject to punishment." He opened the diary Gordon had kept, in which he'd deliberately recorded his curfew violations.

"Were you out after 8:00 p.m. last night?" Manion asked.

"Yes, like you and other Americans," Gordon replied.

"Oh, then you violated the curfew. That would be a 'count two' violation."

Gordon looked Manion in the eye and replied softly, "Are you turning yourself in for curfew violation, since you did exactly as I did, and we are both Americans?"

"Ah, but you are of Japanese ancestry."

"Has the Constitution been suspended?"

Manion had no answer for that. He had not expected an argument. Some of the people being incarcerated had been angry. Some had complained. But none, as far as he knew, had simply refused to cooperate.

Finally, late in the day, Manion took Gordon to the King County Jail in downtown Seattle and left him in the federal holding tank.

On Monday morning, a military officer, Captain Michael Revisto of the Wartime Civil Control Administration, showed up at the jail. Revisto was cordial, even charming, but he was also clearly upset. "You know you violated a lotta things, and if they add these together, you're gonna have a long jail sentence. But they're willing to forget all that. And soon as you sign this statement here, we're all set. I've got a car here ready to take you to Puyallup."

Gordon wanted to be helpful, but he wasn't about to sign the form.

"You know," he said, "I'm not physically objecting to your doing this. It's just that I can't give you the consent myself under the circumstances . . . But I don't see why you can't take me down there *without* my consent. And all you need to do is just get a couple of your guys to escort me down to the car, throw me in the back, and drive down forty miles, open up the barbed wire, plunk me down, drive out, close the gate."

Revisto, startled, replied, "We can't do that!"

"Why not?"

"That'd be breaking the law."

"You mean you think breaking the law, putting me in without signing, is worse than 120,000 people who were forced to be moved out?"[22]

Shaking his head, Revisto gave up and left, perplexed.

On June 1, Gordon was charged in a federal court. He pleaded "not guilty" on the basis that both the exclusion order and the curfew were racially motivated and unconstitutional. He was offered bail, but because he could not be released into the exclusion zone—because he was Japanese American—and because he still refused to register for removal to one of the camps, he was returned to the King County Jail to await trial.

★ ★ ★ ★

For Gordon Hirabayashi in the King County Jail, for Fred Shiosaki in Hillyard, for Rudy Tokiwa in the Salinas Assembly Center, for Kats Miho in Hawai'i, and for thousands of young Japanese Americans like them, the summer and fall of 1942 were seasons of profound discontent and worry.

Many of them and their parents—more than one hundred thousand people—were now living behind barbed-wire fences. Assumptions they had held all their lives had been turned on their heads. Their sense of self, of who they were and how they fit into the larger world, was uncertain. When they washed their faces and combed their hair in the morning, they saw Americans looking back at them from the bathroom mirror. But each and every day they were reminded that many of their compatriots saw them not as Americans but as enemies of all that America stood for and all that they themselves believed in.

There didn't seem to be much they could do about it.

CHAPTER 7

—✕—✕—✕—✕—✕—✕—✕—

EVERY WEEKDAY MORNING, RUDY TOKIWA stood at the perimeter fence of the Salinas Assembly Center, trying to catch a glimpse of his friends as they passed in school buses on their way to Salinas High.

The first day, nearly everyone on the bus saw Rudy, and most waved to him as they passed. A few friends came after school and visited with him through the fence. Some of his football teammates came. The Pozzi brothers came.

Everybody agreed that it just wasn't fair what was happening to Rudy and his family. After all, a lot of them were Italian Americans. Italy was at war with the United States, and they hadn't been locked up.

As the days passed, life on the outside went on, and fewer and fewer kids waved from the bus. Eventually, nobody waved. Rudy realized he was becoming invisible to them. He also realized that he was going to go stir-crazy if he didn't find something to do other than stand staring out through the fence.

At the mess hall one day, he approached Mr. Abe, the head cook. Abe didn't speak much English, but Rudy's Japanese was pretty good. Rudy said that he was bored and that he'd like to learn to cook. Abe, impressed that someone as young as Rudy was willing to put in long hours in the kitchen, didn't hesitate. "I will teach you," he said.

Rudy threw himself into the job. He worked seven days a week, sometimes from 4:00 a.m. until after 8:00 p.m., helping to feed more than a thousand people in a sitting, three times a day. He brewed vats of coffee, poured sacks of rice into enormous pots of boiling water, and scrambled eggs on a griddle—dozens at a time.

Sometimes he wondered whether it might be better to just hang out with the boys who loafed around the camp all day. But Mr. Abe had a way of looking at him and saying, in quick, emphatic Japanese, "If you have free time, your mind wanders and you get in trouble."[23] It reminded Rudy of the stern way his teachers in Japan talked, and while he hadn't liked it then, he found Abe's gruff manner reassuring now. The work, and the discipline it required, helped him cope with the situation. He decided to keep his head down and keep working.

Two months later, the Salinas Assembly Center was closed, and the camp's population transferred to more permanent facilities. On the night of July 4, 1942—Independence Day—Rudy and his family found themselves traveling south, confined to a darkened railway car. Guards had ordered the passengers to pull the window shades down so nobody on the outside caught so much as a glimpse of them as the train passed through the small towns along the route.

The next morning, the passengers stepped off the train into the blast furnace of an Arizona summer. None of them had ever experienced heat like it before. Many of the women were wearing their Sunday best for traveling, and some of the men had on coats and ties. Sweating and bleary-eyed from a mostly sleepless night, they climbed into the backs of green army trucks. Half an hour later, the group arrived at what was to be their home for the foreseeable future: the Poston Relocation Center.

The camp was built on the Colorado River Indian Reservation—home to the Mojave and Chemehuevi people. A tribal council had objected to the camp. They did not want to be a part of an injustice. The government's Office of Indian Affairs had overruled them.

Rudy, squinting against the glare, looked around in disbelief. Row upon row of black, tar paper–clad barracks stood on a vast expanse of sunbaked sand—stretching three miles from one end to the other. Heat waves shimmered, and a fine gray dust lay over everything. The wind was hot and dry and offered no relief. Horned lizards skittered this way and that.

Almost immediately, people began to faint. Those who had arrived earlier rushed to the newcomers, handing out salt tablets and water. Young Nisei women helped others off the backs of the trucks and sat them down in the sand in the narrow margins of shade alongside the barracks. The newly arrived had to sort through mountains of baggage to find their own, then wander through a maze of identical buildings to locate their quarters.

When the Tokiwas found their assigned barracks in Block 213, someone handed Rudy's mother, Fusa, and Fumi empty sacks and pointed to bales of straw outside.

"Fill them up with hay. That's your mattresses."

Fusa and Fumi started stuffing mattresses.

STUFFING MATTRESSES AT POSTON.

It was even hotter inside the building. Drifts of dust had blown up between the floorboards, and Fusa borrowed a broom and started sweeping, but with each gust of hot wind more dust wafted into the room. As in Salinas, there was no furniture, so Rudy and Duke gathered scrap lumber with which to improvise shelving, tables, and chairs. All the new-comers seemed to be doing the same, and all of them were shocked. They had thought that at least there would be beds to sleep in and chairs to sit on.

As evening approached, word spread that although the refrigerators in the mess hall contained food, no one had been assigned to cook. A crowd gathered in front of the kitchen, trying to figure out what to do about it.

Because Rudy had cooked in Salinas, some of the younger men approached him. "Hey, Rudy, how about cookin' here? We gotta have someone cook the meals."

Rudy was irritated. Why him? Why a sixteen-year-old kid? He peered into the kitchen. There was dust and sand on the floor and all over the equipment. "Naw, I ain't going to cook in this heat," he growled. "No way! Any of you guys want to get stuck in there?"

The young men backed off. But they knew Rudy, and they knew how to get to him. A few minutes later, a group of stern-faced older men appeared and, speaking Japanese now, reopened the case.

"We have to have someone cooking, Rudy. And it's going to have to be you young guys. So please, will you take the kitchen over?"

This time Rudy said yes. He didn't like it, but he wasn't one to ignore the wishes of his elders.

Rudy was the right man for the job. He quickly organized a crew and set them to sweeping the place out. When he realized there weren't enough knives and forks, he sent volunteers out to gather wood and begin whittling chopsticks.

But as he looked at the supplies, his anxiety ratcheted up. How was he going to feed hundreds of hungry people with these meager ingredients? It was mostly going to have to be fried Spam. He wasn't looking forward to the complaints.

It was nearly midnight by the time everyone was fed. And, instead of complaining, people thanked Rudy. The old men and women nodded and said, "Dōmo arigatō," thank you very much.

When he finished for the night, Rudy wandered out into the night air. He was proud of what he had done and proud of his people. They were tough, and uncomplaining. As unfair as their situation was, it was nice to feel that he was part

YOUNG MEN PLAYING BASKETBALL AT POSTON.

of a community and able to make things a little better for his companions.

Rudy's first night of cooking soon turned into a full-time job. The WRA employed those incarcerated in the camps to carry on much of the day-to-day business of feeding, policing, educating, caring for, and cleaning up. The pay was low, but it helped people pay off loans on homes they could no longer live in, or their income taxes, or the bills they received for storing their possessions on the outside.

As people settled into life at Poston, they did everything in their power to maintain some sense of normalcy and to combat the boredom—and anger—that threatened to consume them.

They constructed schools, complete with auditoriums, out of adobe bricks they made themselves from mud and straw. They turned spare barracks into Christian and Buddhist churches. They established poultry and hog farms

DUST STORM AT POSTON.

so they could have fresh eggs and meat and irrigated the desert to cultivate crops.

They organized an internal police force and a fire department and ran health clinics, beauty shops, barbershops, and newspapers. They organized Boy Scout troops and PTAs as well as a wide variety of clubs and social activities.

They scraped the sagebrush from the desert to clear baseball diamonds and football fields and set up basketball hoops on the gable ends of barracks. They even smoothed out patches of sand and sank tin cans in them to make "greens" for an improvised desert golf course.

Then they formed sports teams, with leagues and divisions, for baseball, football, basketball, and volleyball. Duke Tokiwa played for Block 213's basketball team, the Terrors. Rudy was athletic, but he was small, not nearly as big and muscular as Duke. Nevertheless, he threw himself into the games wherever he could. Often these games ended abruptly when blinding and choking dust storms swept in off the desert, sending everyone scurrying for the shelter of the barracks with wet cloths clutched to their faces so they could breathe.

Rudy surprised himself by signing up for dancing lessons. He learned to waltz and jitterbug. He resumed his education at the camp's high school and was even asked to teach agricultural classes. He began to make friends among the young men with whom he worked and played—and there were a couple in particular he really looked up to.

There was Lloyd Onoye, who came from the same part of Salinas as Rudy. Lloyd was a gentle giant, so powerful that when he grabbed other young men in wrestling matches or tackled them in football games, he sometimes inadvertently squeezed them so hard they passed out. Lloyd was slow to anger, but once during a basketball game he became enraged over a series of foul calls and wound up dragging six other men around the court as they tried to keep him from throttling the referee. Finally, one of them yelled, "If you want to live, Mac, you'd better get out of here!"

Then there was Harry Madokoro. Harry's father and sister had both died before the war. To make ends meet, Harry worked on a vegetable farm and helped his mother, Netsu, run a candy shop in Watsonville, near where Rudy lived in Salinas. Harry was thirteen years older than Rudy and chief of the camp's internal police force. Thoughtful and sober-minded but always friendly, he commanded a kind of respect that Rudy and the younger men found inspiring and reassuring. When they had squabbles among themselves, they generally sought Harry's counsel, and his counsel almost always proved wise.

By midsummer, Rudy figured he was as content as he was likely to be, living in a desert behind barbed wire against his will. Somehow, against the many obstacles they faced, the residents of Poston had formed a community.

CHAPTER 8

—✕—✕—✕—✕—✕—✕—✕—

SHORTLY BEFORE GORDON HIRABAYASHI'S TRIAL date in
October 1942, a jailer appeared outside his cell with an older
Japanese man. It was a little after midnight, and most of the
men in the cellblock were asleep. Gordon was just drifting
off himself. Then he did a double take. "Hey, that's my dad!"

Gordon had been told that his mother might be summoned to testify in his trial, but he had not expected to see his
father. He was shocked by his father's haggard appearance.

Federal agents had awakened Gordon's father, Shungo
Hirabayashi, and his mother, Mitsu, early that morning at
the Tule Lake camp in Northern California. They'd been traveling all day, and they were exhausted.

Mitsu Hirabayashi had been taken to the women's tank
upstairs. When the cell door closed behind her, she looked
around nervously. Despite the late hour, the room was
brightly lit. Women in green prison uniforms were sitting on
metal benches reading or standing around in clusters, chatting casually as if at an after-church social.

Mitsu noticed an old upright piano in one corner of the room. Some of the keys didn't work, but she sat down and plinked out a tune. Immediately the women gathered around and began to sing. A bit embarrassed by the attention, Mitsu said, "Somebody else play. All I know are some songs like this and church hymns, and you don't want to hear church hymns."

The women replied, "No, no. Nobody plays here. You play."

And so she played, deep into the night, as the women stood behind her and sang along.

The next morning, the jail's matron brought Mitsu a prison uniform and told her to change into it. Mitsu refused. "I'm not a criminal. I'm a witness. I shouldn't be here in the first place."

When the matron persisted, Mitsu demanded to see Gordon's lawyers. The matron quickly backed down, and the other women in the tank looked on with admiration. Mitsu Hirabayashi—like her son—was nobody's fool.

On Tuesday, October 20, Gordon's trial commenced, with Judge Lloyd Llewellyn Black presiding. The case was reported in *The Seattle Times* under a headline that employed a racist term that was widespread at the time: CURFEW TRIAL OF JAP STARTED.

It turned out to be a short and somewhat farcical affair. After the jury was sworn in, the prosecution called Gordon's father to the stand.

Shungo was nervous. He had never been in a courtroom. His English was far from fluent, and his answers, barely audible, were hesitant and unclear.

The judge asked, "Is there anyone here in this place who can interpret for the witness?" Nobody stepped forward.

Gordon looked around the room. The only other Japanese or Japanese American people he saw were his parents. "Well, I can interpret for him," he said, "if you'll accept the defendant."

The judge hesitated but agreed.

Gordon approached the stand. "Where were you born?" the prosecutor asked. Gordon translated the question into Japanese.

His father replied. "In Japan," Gordon translated.

"Do you have any children here in the United States?"

"Yes."

"Is one of them here?"

"Yes."

"Can you point to your son?"

Shungo, looking confused, pointed in Gordon's direction. Gordon smiled, turned to the judge, and said, "Well, in regards to that question, apparently he's confirming that I am his son."

When the prosecution rested, Gordon's attorney, Frank Walters, called Gordon to the stand. Quietly and calmly,

Gordon gave an account of his experiences growing up in America. He'd been educated in public schools, he said. He'd spent much of his teenage years working on his parents' farm, driving tractors and delivery trucks.

He had never been to Japan. He'd been an enthusiastic member of the Boy Scouts of America—an assistant scout master, in fact. He was a Christian, a Quaker most recently. He'd played baseball in high school, was the vice president of the University of Washington YMCA. All in all, he'd had a pretty typical American upbringing.

When the judge dismissed Gordon from the stand, witnesses from the community came forward and testified to his good character. Then Walters rose again. He argued that Executive Order 9066, the subsequent exclusion orders, and the military curfew order deprived Gordon of his liberty without due process of law and thus violated his rights under the Constitution.

When the defense rested, the judge prepared to read the jurors their instructions. He turned to them and said, "You can forget all the talk about the Constitution by the defense. What is relevant here is the public proclamation issued by the Western Defense Command. You are to determine this: Is the defendant a person of Japanese ancestry? If so, has he complied with the military curfew and exclusion orders, which are valid and enforceable laws? It is your duty to accept the law as stated by the Court."[24]

Ten minutes later the jury returned their verdicts: guilty on both counts.

★ ★ ★ ★

At the Hillyard Laundry in Spokane, Washington, the war was much on the minds of the Shiosaki family. Because they lived east of the Columbia River, they were outside the exclusion zone, and for this reason they were not forced to leave their home and business.

But they all feared that at some point Kisaburo might be taken away, as had so many other Issei men. At night, the family sat around the kitchen table making contingency plans. If Kisaburo were to be arrested, Tori and the kids would have to run the laundry themselves.

Fred's older brother, Roy, who ran a laundry in Montana, had been drafted in early January 1942, during a brief period between the attack on Pearl Harbor and when the Selective Service stopped drafting Japanese Americans. Fred resolved that as soon as he turned eighteen, he, too, would follow his brother's lead and sign up. For now, he was keeping that to himself.

At least things were looking up at the laundry. Customers drifted back, and soon they had more business than they could handle. One day, Will Simpson, the newspaper editor, came in carrying a bundle of grubby white work shirts. The family hadn't seen him since the day after Pearl Harbor, when he'd shut his door in Kisaburo's face.

"I can't find anybody to do my shirts right," Simpson said. "Would you do them?"

Kisaburo paused, savoring the moment. Then he put on a mournful face, shook his head sadly, and said, "Jeez, sorry. I'm just too busy."

That August, straight after his eighteenth birthday, Fred took a bus downtown and strode into a Selective Service office, eager to sign up for the US Army. But, living as he did in a mostly white community outside the exclusion zone, he had missed one vital piece of information.

The War Department had decreed that Japanese Americans were ineligible to serve in the US military and were to be classified 4-C—"enemy aliens"—by their local draft boards.

When Fred told the young officer behind the desk that he wanted to enlist, the man stared at him blank-faced for a moment and then said, "You can't sign up. You're an enemy alien."

Stunned, Fred replied, "No, I'm not! I was born in America. I'm a citizen."

"Well, the War Department says you're an enemy alien, so you're an enemy alien."[25]

Fred staggered out onto the sidewalk, shocked and devastated.

As he rode the bus home, he brooded on what had just happened. It defied common sense that a native-born American could be considered either an alien or an enemy, that simply placing the characters *4-C* next to his name on a draft card meant that he couldn't serve his country.

Looking around, he saw that the only people on the bus anywhere near his age were all young women. Nearly all of Spokane's young men were off to war. He sank a little lower in his seat, wishing the driver would hurry up so he could get home.

★ ★ ★ ★

By December 1942, five million US servicemen were away from home, but the military was still straining to build a fighting force large enough and powerful enough to wage war both against Japan in the Pacific and in Europe, where the United States had joined Britain and France in the war against Nazi Germany and its allies.

Ever since Pearl Harbor, Japanese American leaders in Hawai'i and on the mainland had been lobbying the government to allow Nisei men to enlist. It just didn't make sense to have tens of thousands of men idling their time away in Hawai'i or behind barbed-wire fences in the American West.

Beginning in early January 1943, memos began circulating among the War Department, the Selective Service, army intelligence, and the FBI about the possibility of allowing Nisei men to volunteer for a segregated, all–Japanese American combat team.

On February 1, President Roosevelt made it official, signing a memo to the secretary of war, Henry Lewis Stimson, that read, in part, "Americanism is not, and never was, a matter of race or ancestry. A good American is one who is loyal to this country and our creed of liberty and democracy. Every loyal American should be given the opportunity to serve this country."[26]

As soon as Fred Shiosaki heard about the new, all–Japanese American fighting unit, he wasted no time. He took another bus downtown and walked into the same Selective Service office where he had been told he was an enemy alien the previous August.

This time there was a woman sitting behind the desk.

"What's going on?" Fred asked.

The woman smiled and replied, "Well, all you have to do is sign up and you're in."[27] She handed Fred a pen and a piece of paper. He glanced at it, signed, thanked the woman, and headed for home.

The whole thing had taken only minutes. Back at the laundry, Fred paused for a moment before opening the front door. He knew his parents weren't going to take the news well and that his father was going to be angry.

In the Shiosaki family, as in many Japanese American families, the father was the head of the household, the decision maker. Kisaburo would expect to have been consulted about something as momentous as his son going off to war.

Fred took a deep breath, opened the door, nodded at his parents behind the counter of the laundry, and said nothing.

CHAPTER 9

WHEN KATS MIHO HEARD ABOUT the all–Japanese American regiment, he was ablaze with excitement. Since being forced out of the Hawai'i Territorial Guard, he had been working in construction, putting roofs on barracks at the naval air station at Pu'unēnē on Maui. Here at last was his chance to fight for his country.

His older brother, Katsuaki, wanted to enlist too. Katsuaki had been accepted for medical school and was saving money for tuition while working as a paramedic. His dream was to become a doctor and bring much-needed medical services to the plantation towns of rural Maui. But the news about an all–Japanese American regiment had electrified him, too, and in an instant his plans changed.

Kats told his brother that he wanted to be the one to go. That was the last thing Katsuaki wanted to hear. No, he insisted, he would go. The two brothers argued about it for days. Each tried to dissuade the other. Each wanted to take the entire risk upon himself.

The way Kats saw it, someone needed to represent the family in the war effort. Honor demanded it. The Japanese ethics their father had taught them required it, even though the enemy was Japan itself. But his brother shouldn't throw away his future. "You're already accepted to medical school," Kats said. "Your dream is to become a doctor and be a professional."[28]

Katsuaki wasn't buying his brother's argument. It was about more than his dreams or the family honor or even rural Maui's medical needs. It was about conscience and duty.

The dispute simmered for several days, finally culminating in an all-night marathon argument as the brothers sat under the stars in the lush courtyard of the Miho Hotel, surrounded by their mother's orchids. By dawn, they had worn each other down.

They would both go.

Throughout the islands, other young Japanese American men were also eagerly racing to sign up. In some Selective Service offices, there weren't enough typewriters to type up all the paperwork, and more had to be borrowed from local business schools.

The army had called for fifteen hundred Nisei volunteers from Hawai'i. Nearly ten thousand answered that call.

Late in the afternoon on March 28, 1943, the first group of newly enlisted Nisei soldiers assembled on the grounds of Honolulu's 'Iolani Palace for a formal aloha ceremony. Kats

FAREWELL CEREMONY FOR NISEI VOLUNTEERS AT 'IOLANI PALACE.

and Katsuaki Miho were among the twenty-six hundred men standing in ranks, wearing crisp new khaki uniforms and white leis around their necks.

Nearly twenty thousand onlookers crowded into the palace grounds, climbing into the banyan trees, craning their necks to catch a glimpse of the soldiers. Overhead, fairy terns circled in dazzling white loops in the sky. An artillery band played on the bandstand, and the Royal Hawaiian Glee Club sang the Hawaiian anthem, "Hawai'i Pono'ī."

Officials made long-winded speeches thanking the new soldiers for what they were about to do, but the mayor of Honolulu spoke only briefly, saying, "I know you young men well enough to know you don't want a fuss made over you."[29]

On April 5, they moved out and marched in a rough column down King Street toward Honolulu's Pier 7. Once again, thousands of friends and family came to see them off. Mothers and wives and sisters and aunties brought bento boxes full of treats that they tried to hand to the men as they marched by, staggering under overstuffed duffel bags.

Daniel Inouye later remembered, "We were not soldiers at that point. Our uniforms didn't fit, and we carried ukuleles and guitars and all kinds of things like that, very unmilitary-like . . . We looked like prisoners."[30]

The luxury liner SS *Lurline* was waiting for them at the harbor, painted battleship gray to make it less visible to Japanese submarines. Cabins intended for two housed as many as twelve, with bunks stacked two and three high against every available wall.

As the ship departed, the men stood on deck, watching the Aloha Tower, a Honolulu landmark, recede in the distance. They did not yet know how often and how keenly they would think of it in the months to come, how they would long to see it and the fairy terns circling above the city and, beyond them, the lovely green mountains wreathed in white clouds.

As soon as they were at sea, Kats became violently sea-sick. His small, dark cabin reeked of sweaty clothes, diesel fumes, and vomit—all of which made him feel even worse. He remained in his bunk, moaning and retching, for most of the next four and a half days. The ship followed the same zigzag course toward San Francisco as the ship that took his father to imprisonment on the mainland the previous year.

The weather grew blustery, cold, and gray, and Kats sank even deeper into the misery of seasickness. But when the ship finally passed under the Golden Gate Bridge, he joined his brother and the other men on the deck to gaze up at it. San Francisco was the biggest city most of them had ever

NISEI SOLDIERS ON A TRAIN TO CAMP SHELBY.

seen, and they tried to soak in all the sights—the notorious prison on Alcatraz, the elegant Victorian homes along the waterfront, the Ferry Building.

A few days later, they boarded a troop train, and their officers told them for the first time where they were going: Camp Shelby, near Hattiesburg, Mississippi. Henceforth they were to consider themselves members of the 442nd Regimental Combat Team (RCT), an all–Japanese American fighting unit.

★ ★ ★ ★

In Poston, as in all ten of the mainland concentration camps, the reaction to the news that the Nisei could now enlist was very different than it had been in Hawai'i. Viewed from behind barbed wire, the invitation to fight and die for America struck many as less than tempting. For some, it was downright insulting.

The US Army organized a question-and-answer session at Poston as a first step in recruiting as many Nisei soldiers as possible out of the camp. Nearly two thousand young men and their families crowded into the auditorium to hear what the army representative, Lieutenant John Bolton, had to say.

Bolton addressed mostly practical concerns: When would inductions begin? Would the Nisei soldiers be fighting the Germans in Europe or the Japanese in the South Pacific? Could their parents receive their paychecks? What ranks and pay grades would be open to them?

But Bolton had no answers for the larger, more troubling

questions. Why should Nisei men lay their lives on the line for a country that forced them and their parents to live in concentration camps? If they fought for America, would America release their family members, grant their parents citizenship, and restore their civil rights? Why would the all–Japanese American fighting unit be a segregated unit, like the Black 92nd Division?

There was another major sticking point. Bolton said that every adult in the camps was now required to sign a loyalty oath, whether or not they planned to enlist. Why was that required of them and not of other Americans?

For many of the young men at Poston—and for their sisters, wives, mothers, and fathers, as well—it just didn't add up.

After the meeting, Rudy and his friends huddled together, arguing about signing up, unable to come to an agreement. They needed to figure it out. Registration would take place at the end of the week, just four days away. Lloyd Onoye called for a meeting of their own. Every young man sixteen and older, he said, should attend.

The next morning, they gathered out in the desert, where a few mesquite trees offered a scant bit of shade. About forty men showed up. They formed a rough circle, some sitting on boulders, some leaning against the twisted black tree trunks.

Then Harry Madokoro stepped into the middle of the circle and got things going. As far as he was concerned, he said, they should all sign up and do it right away, but he wanted to hear what the others thought.

One young man piped up. "Why should we go out, fight for a country that locks us up?" Others nodded their heads in agreement.

Harry got up again and said that he was going to volunteer anyway. It wasn't a choice, he said. It was a duty. Besides, it was also an opportunity. When the war was over, either they would return from the camps still stigmatized as "Japs" or they would return as Americans who had served, maybe even as war heroes.

Lloyd Onoye said he was in, too. Most of the younger men were still skeptical.

Finally, Rudy stood up. He was the youngest there, and in

PRIVATE RUDY TOKIWA.

some ways he was more "Japanese" than many of the others, being fluent in the language and having gone to school in Japan. But he wasn't Japanese. He was an American. An angry one. That's what it came down to for him now. He deserved respect. His father and his mother deserved respect. His sister deserved respect. And if he had to fight to earn respect, he'd fight.

"Say nobody volunteers out of the camps," Rudy said. "What can Roosevelt say? Well, he can say that we're more loyal to Japan than the United States, that's what."

A consensus slowly formed, and by the time the meeting broke up, nearly every man there had committed to registering by the end of the week.

★ ★ ★ ★

It couldn't be put off any longer. A letter arrived informing Fred Shiosaki that he was to report to Fort Douglas in Utah for induction into the army. He waited until his parents were together in the kitchen, then sauntered into the room and told them the news as casually as he could.

His father stared at him for a moment. Then he exploded in a torrent of Japanese curses that Fred couldn't understand. He went on and on. Fred was afraid he was going to hit him. He'd never seen him so angry.

But the more his father yelled, the more determined Fred became. He was eighteen now, and he could make his own decisions. He didn't need anyone's approval, not even his parents', much as he respected them.

PRIVATE FRED SHIOSAKI.

A few days later, his sister, Blanche, drove him to the train station. Kisaburo refused to go, refused even to say goodbye. Weeks later, Private First Class Shiosaki was back in Hillyard, wearing a crisp new khaki uniform. The army had conducted his physical, given him his inoculations, run some aptitude tests, and told him it would be a few more weeks before he'd get orders to report to basic training in Mississippi. To fill the interval, Fred went back to work in the laundry.

But when the day came to leave, Kisaburo Shiosaki drove his son to the station. As the train pulled in, he took Fred's hand, shook it, looked him in the eye, and said, simply, "Come back healthy."[31]

Then, without another word, he turned around and walked away.

Soon after that, a service flag with two blue stars appeared in the downstairs front window of the Hillyard Laundry. A tradition begun in World War I, the flag indicated the number of family members serving in the military. If the worst happened and the family member was killed, the blue star would be replaced with one of gold.

CHAPTER 10

—✕—✕—✕—✕—✕—✕—✕—

GORDON HIRABAYASHI CONTINUED TO WAGE his own quiet war on behalf of his principles. Early on the morning of February 12, 1943, he walked out of the King County Jail and onto Seattle's bustling Third Avenue. His attorneys had taken his case to the Supreme Court and organized bail so he could live in Spokane while waiting for a ruling on his case.

Gordon found lodgings in Spokane with some fellow Quakers, then went to meet his principal mentor, Floyd Schmoe—a Quaker activist as well as an accomplished mountaineer and marine biologist.

Shortly after Pearl Harbor, Schmoe resigned from a faculty position at the University of Washington to devote his time to championing the rights of incarcerated Issei and Nisei. From the beginning, he had been one of Gordon's fiercest defenders and advocates.

Schmoe's daughter, Esther, a nursing student and a Quaker activist like her father, was a vibrant young woman with blond curls, a sprinkle of freckles, and luminous blue eyes. She was also intelligent, sociable, and brimming over with youthful hope and idealism.

Esther visited Gordon weekly while he was in jail, first in the company of her father and then increasingly by herself—just her and Gordon sitting on cold metal benches, talking through the bars, sharing their ideas about life and religion, and falling in love.

Now Gordon helped Esther and her father set up the new American Friends Service Committee office, and the three went to work trying to ease the burdens of Japanese American families in the Pacific Northwest—both those in the camps and those outside the exclusion zone.

One day, Esther was in a Spokane laundry, inquiring about possible jobs for people she was trying to help. Gordon waited for her in the car. At first, all went well. The owner had several positions and was ready to hire—until he found out that Esther was representing Japanese Americans. He exploded. "Hell no! We don't want to take a chance hiring Japanese!"[32]

When Esther got back to the car, she wept for five minutes straight. Until then, she had not quite realized what she was up against. Gordon, comforting her, hadn't realized how different the world looked through her eyes.

For him, that kind of treatment was nothing new. Just recently, he'd been traveling with a white friend in Idaho when they decided to stop at a restaurant in a dusty little farm town called Caldwell. They failed to notice the sign in the front window—NO JAPS.

A waitress came over and took their order, but half an hour went by, and no food appeared. Finally, the waitress edged back to the table and asked Gordon, "Are you Japanese?"

"No, I'm American. I'm of Japanese ancestry, but I'm American."

"Oh, well, if you're of Japanese ancestry, we can't serve you."

Gordon asked to speak to the manager. The man seemed nervous, almost apologetic. "I'm forced to do it," he said. "If I don't, I'll have people boycotting me, walking out."

Gordon didn't get angry, and he didn't argue. Instead, he proposed an experiment. "Well, you have an empty table right near the entrance. Let me test whether you're correct or not . . . If anybody comes in, sees me, and leaves, I'll pay for an average meal so that you wouldn't have lost that."

The man hesitated. Gordon persisted, logically and patiently making his case. "I want to test this," he said. "I'm curious myself."

The manager agreed warily to the deal, but only if Gordon sat at the counter, not near the door. Gordon and his friend ate as slowly as they could and managed to run another hour off the clock. Nothing happened. No one got up and left. No one seemed to even notice. Gordon paid up, and they left. A few weeks later, Gordon's friend wrote to him from Idaho. "Say, that guy took that sign off."[33]

For weeks, Gordon had been growing more impatient to know that his case had been resolved by the Supreme Court. He had no doubt that he would win. The racial rationale behind the curfew was so obvious, the lack of due process leading to the incarcerations so apparent, that neither could possibly fit within the framework of the Constitution.

When the court finally rendered its opinion in *Hirabayashi v. United States*, on June 21, Gordon only learned of it from the newspapers. What he read there was crushing. The justices, acting unanimously, backed the government's assertion that wartime conditions justified the racist policy. Gordon couldn't believe it. He later wrote, "I thought that the raison d'être for the Supreme Court was to uphold the Constitution. I didn't realize the extent to which World War II hysteria had swept up everyone."[34]

Now all he could do was keep busy working with his Quaker colleagues and wait for someone to show up and take him back to jail.

It wasn't until September that a big black sedan pulled up and an FBI agent approached Gordon and asked him if he knew where Gordon Hirabayashi was.

"I am he," Gordon replied. "What took you so long?"[35]

When Gordon arrived downtown, there was a hitch. He had agreed to accept a longer sentence—ninety days rather than sixty—so he'd be eligible to do his time in a federal work camp rather than in another crowded jail. That way, he figured, he'd at least be outdoors and doing something productive.

The FBI agents told him that wasn't going to work. The closest work camp was Fort Lewis, near Tacoma, well within the exclusion zone, which legally Gordon could not enter. The next closest was in Tucson, Arizona, and the government wasn't about to pay to send him there. He'd have to serve his time in the Spokane County Jail.

Gordon unleashed his customary firm, implacable logic. He pointed out that the government was violating its agreement with him. If they couldn't afford to send him to Tucson, that wasn't his fault. Why not let him get himself to Arizona? Supposing he just hitchhiked?

The agent in charge was surprised by the proposal, but Gordon wore him down with his calm but relentless manner of arguing. Finally the agent shrugged and approved the idea, and Gordon set out for Arizona.

Traveling first to Idaho and then through eastern Oregon into Utah and Nevada, he trudged for endless miles alongside remote highways, his thumb stuck out, as cars and trucks sped by. Sometimes drivers slowed down, saw that he was Asian, and sped up again. Occasionally, someone took him a few miles down the road.

A farmer driving a truck picked Gordon up, studied him

for a while out of the corner of his eye as he drove, and finally said, "You're a Chinese, right?"

"No, I'm an American."

"I know that, but you're a Chinese American, aren't you?"

"My parents came from Japan."

The farmer chewed on that for a few moments, then replied, "If I'd known that, I wouldn't have picked you up."

Gordon offered to get out of the truck, but the man grudgingly kept driving. After a long silence, they began to chat, then to talk in earnest. Gordon explained why he was on his way to prison, what he believed in, how proud he was to be an American, and what the Constitution meant to him. The farmer ended up inviting Gordon to his home, drawing him a warm bath, feeding him dinner, and then driving him to a well-traveled road so he could continue on his way.

When Gordon finally got to Tucson, he walked into the office of the local federal marshal. The marshal was perplexed by the sudden appearance of this strange young man. At first, he tried to get rid of him. "What's your name? We don't have any orders to take you in, so you might as well go home."

Gordon wasn't having any of that. "It took me a couple of weeks to get down here, and I'd go home, but you'd probably find those orders and I would have to do this all again."[36] He suggested the marshal make some phone calls.

The marshal told him to come back that evening, and

Gordon wandered outside into the blistering heat. He found an air-conditioned movie theater and settled in to watch a show. By the time he returned, the marshal had made the calls, decided Gordon was in fact a legitimate lawbreaker, and agreed to incarcerate him.

A deputy drove Gordon out into the foothills and delivered him to the Catalina Federal Honor Camp. There, inside the gates, standing silently among scraggly pines, mesquite trees, and rock formations aglow in an Arizona sunset, stood a small contingent of inmates who had heard that the famous Gordon Hirabayashi was coming. They wanted to welcome him personally.

CHAPTER 11

✕ ✕ ✕ ✕ ✕ ✕ ✕

THAT APRIL, KATS AND THE Nisei soldiers from Hawai'i arrived in Hattiesburg, Mississippi. During the three-day train ride across the country, they were allowed off the train only twice—in the middle of the night and in open countryside where no one would see them.

At Camp Shelby, just south of town, they were assigned hutments—long, narrow sheds set up off the ground. The spring weather in Mississippi was freezing by Hawaiian standards, and they huddled next to coal-burning stoves or lay on their metal cots, shivering under green wool army blankets.

The water in the showers had only one temperature—cold. The roofs were leaky. The latrines were open ditches, and they stank. The food—mutton, boiled potatoes, mushy peas, pork and beans, creamed beef on toast—was unfamiliar. Most of the men, used to eating fresh fruit, fresh fish, and rice, found nearly all of it vile. By the end of the first week, some of them could be found crouched behind the hutments, homesick and weeping.

But the biggest obstacle wasn't the living conditions, or the food, or homesickness. It was each other.

The men from Hawai'i weren't the first Nisei troops to arrive in Shelby. Another group of Nisei, from the mainland, was there before them. This first group had already gone through basic training, and they occupied nearly all the non-commissioned officer positions. They were the corporals, the sergeants, the staff sergeants.

The men from Hawai'i found themselves having to take orders from men who looked like them, who had surnames like theirs, whose ancestry was the same as theirs, but who spoke and acted as if they were from an entirely different world.

Then more mainland men showed up from the concentration camps out west, and an already tense situation got worse. Fistfights broke out all over camp. The islanders called the mainlanders "kotonks," after the hollow sound a coconut makes when it is hit. They claimed that's what the mainlanders' heads sounded like when they hit them. The mainlanders started referring to the men from Hawai'i as "Buddhaheads," though no one on either side was sure what that meant.

They couldn't even have a conversation without it turning into a fight. The men from Hawai'i spoke a hybrid language, Hawaiian Pidgin, which sounded coarse or even ignorant to the mainlanders. It was neither. It was a warm, familiar language that combined words and expressions from English, Portuguese, Hawaiian, Cantonese, Japanese, Korean, Tagalog, and Spanish.

When a Buddhahead told a kotonk, "You go stay go," he would become irritated when the mainlander didn't understand that he was being told to "go ahead and leave." And the mainlander would be irritated because he just plain didn't understand.

At first, many of the mainlanders let their contempt show. George Goto, from Colorado, thought the men from Hawai'i didn't even speak or understand English. Chester Tanaka, from St. Louis, thought they were "savages." The mainlanders laughed at the way the islanders talked. But laughing was the worst thing they could do—guaranteed to set off a melee.

Language wasn't the only problem. The mainlanders who volunteered from the concentration camps arrived angry, determined to prove themselves as patriotic Americans. They were clean-cut and respectful of authority—as their parents had taught them to be. The Buddhaheads, on the other hand, were happy-go-lucky and approached life as an adventure. They carried ukuleles and guitars wherever they went, danced and sang whenever they could, and were warmly affectionate with one another. They had grown up together and thought of one another as belonging to the same 'ohana— the same big family.

And they tended to see authority—particularly any kind

of authority that seemed designed to hold them down—as something to be defied at every turn.

This defiance came from a deep place—from their own and their Issei parents' experience in Hawai'i. They knew what their parents had endured at the hands of the mostly white and powerful owners and managers on the sugarcane and pineapple plantations. They also knew what they themselves had experienced growing up in a racially and economically stratified society. And they weren't about to put up with a bunch of Japanese American men their own age who sounded and acted like the white bosses back home.

Shortly after arriving at Shelby, Kats Miho was assigned to the 442nd's dedicated artillery unit, the 522nd Field Artillery Battalion. He spent a lot of his time in classrooms, learning the complex geometry and calculus required to accurately fire the unit's big howitzer cannons.

This did nothing, though, to insulate him from the war between the kotonks and the Buddhaheads. He already knew many of the men from Maui, and he was as comfortable speaking Hawaiian Pidgin as standard English.

But Kats occupied the middle ground. He tended to hang out with other former university students, whether from the University of Hawai'i or schools on the mainland. And he always preferred to fight with strong, logical arguments rather than with his fists.

HULA AT SHELBY.

One of the university students Kats grew close to, also assigned to the 522nd, was George Oiye from Montana. George had been born in a cabin in the woods, the nearest store twelve hours away on snowshoes. Like most Montana boys, he grew up with a hunting rifle in one hand and a fishing rod in the other.

George had been popular in high school, playing quarterback on the football team and mingling easily with the nearly all-white student body. He dreamed of becoming an aviator in the army and began taking engineering classes.

Then came Pearl Harbor.

George tried to enlist, but, like Fred Shiosaki, he was told that he was an "enemy alien." He persisted, determined to get into the army and fly airplanes. He argued his case to some of his professors, who went repeatedly to the adjutant general of Montana State University's ROTC program, lobbying on George's behalf.

Finally, one day in early 1943, his earnestness and his popularity on campus paid off. The adjutant general called George into his office and told him that if he could get five prominent white townspeople to vouch for his loyalty, he could enlist in the army and train as an aviator.

It seemed terribly unfair to George that he should have to have white people vouch for him, but he quickly secured the recommendations. The town threw him a going-away party, and soon he was on his way to Fort Douglas in Utah to be processed into the service.

It was only after he was sworn in that someone told him he wasn't going to be flying any planes. Instead, he was to report to a place called Camp Shelby for training as an infantryman.

George was shocked and angry. He felt betrayed.

Things only got worse when he got to Mississippi. Having been in the ROTC program, George knew how to wear his uniform properly. He kept his shoes polished and his shirts buttoned to the collar. He snapped to attention when officers entered a room. He made up his bunk according to regulations.

The men from Hawai'i, who went barefoot as often as they could and wore their uniform shirts open to the waist when it was hot, hated George's spit-and-polish ways and beat him up every chance they got.

George needed friends, preferably those who spoke like the men from Hawai'i. He gravitated toward Kats, and Kats readily offered both his friendship and his protection. It was a friendship that would only grow stronger as time passed and both men experienced the hazards of war.

CHAPTER 12

—✕—✕—✕—✕—✕—✕—✕—

DESPITE THE CONTINUING CONFLICT, THAT spring, as the weather warmed and the dogwoods blossomed in the woods around them, the Nisei men learned the fundamentals of soldiering. Wearing uniforms that were often too large for them and helmets that sometimes hung down below their ears, they drilled for endless hours on the parade grounds.

They ran obstacle courses, dug the small defensive pits known as foxholes, endured early morning bed inspections, disassembled and reassembled their rifles over and over again, cleaned out latrines, and peeled vast numbers of potatoes.

Then it began to rain, and the red Mississippi dust turned into red Mississippi mud. The men were made to get down on their bellies and crawl through it, clutching their rifles, wriggling under barbed wire as someone fired machine-gun rounds over their heads.

Then, on June 15, the 100th Infantry Battalion—another unit of all-Nisei soldiers from Hawai'i who had enlisted or been drafted before Pearl Harbor—returned to Shelby from maneuvers. For Kats and many of the 442nd's Buddhaheads, it was a joyous occasion.

Young men who had known one another as boys on the islands renewed old friendships and exchanged family news. They got out ukuleles and sat on the steps of their hutments singing island songs. To the 442nd men, the 100th soldiers were like big brothers, whom they looked up to with respect and a measure of awe. They were mostly a few years older and had been in the service for at least a year and a half. They walked and talked with a certain amount of swagger and confidence.

By midsummer, the men of the 442nd had completed their basic training and were heading off on their first furloughs. Many of the Buddhaheads had been given large stashes of cash by their parents, who were eager for their sons to have a good time before they went off to war. They climbed onto trains and buses bound for New Orleans and New York City in high spirits.

The kotonks, on the other hand, were not so flush. Most of them were sending money from their paychecks to their parents in the camps to purchase small comforts and conveniences, and most of them, as soon as they had leave, headed for the camps to visit their families behind barbed wire.

Not everyone in the camps was pleased to see Nisei in uniform. Some of their fathers and brothers and uncles took them to one side and told them they were fools for enlisting, for being tools of an American government that was oppressing their people. For the most part, the young soldiers remained steadfast, convinced of the rightness of their actions.

But they headed back to Camp Shelby disturbed and angry, having been reminded of what their families were enduring in the camps.

Refreshed from their furloughs, the Buddhaheads could not understand why the kotonks were always so serious. The kotonks thought the men from Hawai'i frivolous and undisciplined, clueless about what was going on in the country. As morale continued to spiral downward and the fighting continued, the senior officer corps wondered whether the Japanese American soldiers would ever come together as an effective fighting unit. Should they just dissolve the regiment?

Nearly all the 442nd's commissioned officers were white, with only a small number of Japanese Americans in leadership positions, mostly doctors and chaplains. To the Buddhaheads, the army's racial hierarchy—white men at the top, everybody else working for them—mirrored the way in which the plantations back home were run. To the kotonks, it mirrored the way the camps where their families were incarcerated were run.

But as they got to know them, both the kotonks and the Buddhaheads began to warm to their officers. The fact was that most of the 442nd's white officers made a deliberate choice to join the unit. They *wanted* to go into battle with Japanese Americans, and they were prepared to die with them.

The notion that these white officers would voluntarily share the hazards of war with them impressed the Nisei. And before long it was clear that the respect and goodwill were mutual.

The commander of the 442nd was Colonel Charles Wilbur Pence. Short, blunt-faced, and tough as a rooster, Pence made it clear right from the start of basic training that the men were in for a rough time. Then he sat down and penned a heartfelt letter to each of their mothers: "You have given a soldier to the Army of the United States. He has arrived here safely, and I am happy to have him in my command . . . We shall make a glorious record for the Japanese Americans in our country."[37]

It was the "we" that mattered to the men. It came through in everything Pence did and said. He made it clear that he personally would be leading them into battle, putting his life on the line along with theirs. He seldom pulled rank, played baseball on the camp diamond with them, and enjoyed chatting with them in the mess hall. Pence believed in them and in what they were trying to do. And, before long, they believed in him.

In August, the 100th packed their duffel bags, said their alohas, and left Shelby, bound for North Africa, Italy, and the war.

The 442nd men were sad to see them go. Most had finished basic training by now and faced testing and field trials to prove their competency in everything from marksmanship to physical fitness. Almost without exception, they excelled, with 98 percent of them earning passing scores—the highest average in the entire Third Army that summer.

In early September, some of the army's top officers arrived for a formal review. In full battle uniforms, amid the clashing of cymbals and the blaring of brass, the Nisei soldiers—infantrymen, engineers, medics, and artillerymen—unfurled the Stars and Stripes, hoisted their regimental colors, and marched past their officers in tight, crisp formations. As the last company of the "Go for Broke" regiment—as they had begun to call themselves—stepped off the field, Pence turned to a reporter from the *Honolulu Star-Bulletin* and said, with a jut to his jaw and a glint in his eye, "I'll take these men into battle without hesitation."[38]

The fact was, Pence was coming to love these young men. But he was still struggling to get them to stop fighting each other. He had demoted men for fighting. He'd even threatened to disband the entire outfit. Nothing had worked.

When two Japanese American chaplains arrived at Camp Shelby, Pence gave them the urgent task of finding a way forward.

Both Chaplain Hiro Higuchi and Chaplain Masao Yamada were from Hawai'i. They had watched with admiration but deep concern when thousands of island men signed up to serve, and they both decided they needed to accompany these men to war, to watch out for them on the battlefield.

It was Hiro Higuchi who found a solution to the conflict.

Higuchi noticed that the Buddhaheads were always talking about what their homecoming after the war would be like: the parades, the lū'aus, the leis hung around their necks, home-cooked meals, falling asleep in their own beds to the sound of pounding surf and rustling palms.

Most of the mainlanders, many of whom had come out of the camps, had nothing like that to look forward to. For some of them, there might not even be homes to return to. At best there would be a scramble to find land to farm, a struggle to rent houses in segregated neighborhoods, and the huge effort required to help parents start new businesses, all amid the continued scorn of many of their neighbors. At worst, there might be a return to the misery of camps.

Higuchi realized that the men from Hawai'i had no idea what the mainlanders were dealing with. Some of them had never even heard about the concentration camps. Perhaps, he figured, if the Buddhaheads saw the camps for themselves, they might begin to understand the mainlanders and ease up on them.

He went to Pence and proposed a series of organized trips. Pence immediately agreed. Send as many of the men from Hawai'i as you can, he said, especially the leaders and the opinion formers. Kats Miho was a natural choice. So was Daniel Inouye.

They left early in the morning. As the buses rolled north through a vast sea of white cotton, the ukuleles and guitars came out, and the men began to sing and horse around. Everyone was in high spirits. They had no idea where they were going.

Then they came around a bend in the road and saw what appeared to be some kind of military camp up ahead. They had arrived at the Jerome Relocation Center, in southeastern Arkansas.

Kats piled off the bus with the others and found himself looking through tall fencing at row upon row of flimsy barracks made from tar paper and pinewood. Guard towers stood at the gate and on the four corners of the compound.

And the guns in the towers were pointed inward, at the people moving around inside the fence. Japanese and Japanese American people, like them. Realization slowly dawned on the men. Kats was shocked. They were all shocked.

Kats couldn't believe what he was seeing. These were American citizens, like himself. There were women and small children—girls playing hopscotch, a boy bouncing a rubber ball against a wall. A pregnant woman passed, carrying a basket of laundry. Middle-aged men sat idle on the steps of a barracks, staring blankly back at them. Their expressions weren't frightened or angry so much as dull, impassive, as if they had given up, had nothing to look forward to.

Most of the families did their best to welcome the Nisei soldiers. They had saved up their rations of food and used their communal kitchens to prepare small feasts. They presented gifts—mostly kobu, traditional wood carvings they had made from the twisted roots of oak and swamp cypress trees. They offered to sleep outside so the soldiers could sleep in the barracks, but the men said they'd do fine sleeping on the bus or in the mess hall.

On the bus ride back to Mississippi, nobody pulled out musical instruments. For the most part, there was silence. The men wanted time to think about what they had seen. They could not help but wonder if they would have volunteered for the army out of such a place.

When they got back to Shelby, they told the other men from Hawai'i to go and see the camps for themselves. And with each busload that returned, more Buddhaheads began to ease up on more kotonks.

After visiting one of the camps, one of the Buddhaheads approached Rudy Tokiwa, eager to tell him about his visit. "Hey, Rudy, all you mainland guys. Your families in places like that?"

"Well, majority of 'em, yes."

"Well, how much money these guys gettin' paid to be in there?"

"They don't get paid."

"Hey, you kotonks good up in the head, yeah? You be buddies with everybody?"[39]

The war between the kotonks and the Buddhaheads was finally beginning to wind down.

CHAPTER 13

—✗—✗—✗—✗—✗—✗—✗—

OVER TIME, INCARCERATED ISSEI, SUCH as Katsuichi Miho, were brought before hearing boards. Some were given permission to join their families in the concentration camps. Most of the rest were moved from one military facility to another as the government tried to figure out the most cost-effective way to keep them—along with increasing numbers of Italian, German, and Japanese prisoners of war (POWs)—behind barbed wire.

When Kats Miho and his brother Katsuaki enlisted, the Department of Justice suggested that their father might be eligible to be released into the legal custody of his sons. But Katsuichi refused to leave unless roughly twenty other Maui Issei incarcerated with him were also allowed to go home to Hawai'i.

So, instead of being released, he was moved to Fort Missoula, in Montana, in June 1943.

The air in Montana was fresh and cool. At night, brilliant sprays of stars lit up a vast and utterly black sky. By day, from almost anywhere in camp, there were spectacular views of the jagged Bitterroot Mountains.

But boredom and tedium filled the Issei men's days. With little else to do, they collected and patiently polished by hand the stones they dug from the camp's soil—mostly agates, jasper, and jadeite—before carving them into figurines, ashtrays, jewelry, soap dishes. The work passed the time and soothed the soul.

Sometimes, the men were allowed to fish in the Bitterroot River that flowed through a corner of the camp. They caught trout and whitefish, which they sliced into sashimi, or ate fried, or sometimes smoked to send to relatives on the outside.

Katsuichi began to feel that perhaps his fate was not quite so grim as he had feared when he was led away from his home at gunpoint. He missed Ayano and his children desperately. He missed the Miho Hotel and his busy life in Kahului. He worried about his daughters living in Japan. He still thought of himself as Japanese, but he was proud that two of his sons had volunteered for the US Army. He never doubted that they should serve their country. That was the way of the samurai, after all: to faithfully serve those to whom one owed loyalty, even at the cost of one's life.

So now, here in the mountains of Montana, he would wait out the war as patiently as he could and let younger men settle the dispute between nations. He would gather and polish colorful stones like the other old men and look forward to the day when his family would be reunited.

✦ ✦ ✦ ✦

As they graduated from basic training, some of the Nisei soldiers from Camp Shelby were sent to Alabama to guard German POWs captured in North Africa. The Germans had eagerly volunteered to dig peanuts on private farms—largely to escape the boredom of sitting in camps. With thousands of Black farm laborers serving in the military, Alabama's peanut farmers were glad to have the help.

In many rural communities, particularly in the South, the German prisoners—all white men—were not only tolerated but sometimes even welcomed, sharing Sunday dinner with local families, or eating at lunch counters and drinking from water fountains where Black Americans were not allowed to eat or drink. The locals often seemed more at ease with the German prisoners than the Japanese Americans guarding them, even though not long before those same Germans had been doing their best to kill Americans.

But guarding the Germans proved to be an exceptionally easy duty for the Nisei soldiers. By and large, the POWs were friendly, easygoing, and happy to be out of the war. They hadn't the slightest interest in escaping.

The Nisei sat in the shade under trees watching the Germans dig peanuts. Many didn't even bother to load their rifles. At least once, a soldier handed his loaded rifle to a

POW so he could shoot some crows that were gobbling the peanuts as fast as they could dig them.

Among the men guarding Germans in Alabama was Kats's brother Katsuaki. One September night, he and roughly twenty other guards were returning to their base after visiting a movie theater when their truck overturned as the driver took a bend in the road a little too fast.

The soldiers were catapulted from the back of the truck. Some landed in the grass beside the road. Some slammed into the asphalt roadway. More than a dozen were injured, and two were killed instantly: Private Shosei Kutaka and Corporal Katsuaki Miho.

No news could have been harder for Kats to bear. He was exceptionally close to Katsuaki and looked up to him as little brothers often look up to big brothers. He was devastated.

★ ★ ★ ★

As the fall of 1943 slid toward winter and the weather cooled again in Mississippi, the men of the 442nd spent little time at Camp Shelby. They were mostly out in the woods now, living in pup tents or sleeping under the stars on beds of pine boughs or in dank foxholes.

Fred Shiosaki's feet hurt nearly all the time, but he was so fit he could march all day with fifty pounds of gear on his back and hardly break a sweat. Rudy Tokiwa slogged along, uncomplaining, lean, lithe, and tougher than ever, grateful for the time he had spent on long marches as a boy in Japan.

More and more, the men grew comfortable in their individual jobs. More and more, they worked together seamlessly, moving through the woods not as individuals but as squads and platoons, as part of something larger than themselves.

They didn't realize it yet, but they were becoming one of the most proficient and deadly fighting forces in the Third Army.

And, for the first time, they began to have fun in the woods. In their free time, they foraged for wild persimmons and pecans. At night, they lay on their backs, staring at the stars and talking story. They played practical jokes on each other, and particularly on their officers.

More and more, they were speaking the same language. Men who'd grown up in the American West surrounded by sagebrush—like George Oiye and Fred Shiosaki—now sounded as if they'd grown up on Hawai'i surrounded by cane fields. Hawaiian Pidgin, the language that had at first divided them so sharply, was becoming their shared language, knitting the 442nd together, defining the contours of their identity.

Almost every night, the men from Hawai'i pulled out their ukuleles and guitars and sang island songs with sweet voices, their words floating improbably through the night air over moonlit bayous.

And now there was something new. The kotonks were joining in.

As they sat around their campfires, they began to talk about what was to come. What the war would be like when they finally got into it. What it would feel like to be wounded or to die on the battlefield. What they would suffer or what their parents or siblings would suffer when they got the bad news. They worried about that.

But most of all they worried that the war might end before they got into battle. That would be worse than dying, they agreed. They would lose forever the chance to prove their loyalty and earn Japanese Americans their rightful place in American society.

They talked about what was happening in Europe, where Germany, ruled by the fascist Nazi Party and its leader, Adolf Hitler, had in 1939 and 1940 invaded its neighbors, bringing about war with Britain and France. They talked about why that mattered in America. They came back again and again to what they had learned in high school about the American Constitution and the principles of democracy: personal liberty, equality, free speech, the right to vote for their leaders. They talked about whether those things could be said to exist in a country that imprisoned their families.

They also talked about the values their Japanese parents had taught them. Fred talked about the expectation in his family that he and his siblings would always respect their parents' authority and uphold the family's honor.

Kats talked about the samurai movies he used to watch

as a boy and how he had learned from them the eight virtues of Bushido, the warrior's code: rectitude, courage, benevolence, politeness, honesty, honor, loyalty, and self-control. He talked about his father's emphasis on giri, social obligation, and balancing it with ninjō, human warmth and compassion.

Rudy talked about his boyhood military training in Japan, about the idea of gaman—enduring the seemingly unendurable quietly and with patience—and about the spirit of Yamato-damashii, sticking together no matter what, fighting for your group rather than for yourself.

As they talked these things over among themselves, something solid and enduring began to take shape—a common identity that was both American and Japanese, something that, in the not-too-distant future, would carry them through unimaginable hardships and terrors.

Finally, on April 22, 1944, the order came, and the men were assigned to their battalions and companies. Fred and Rudy were both placed in the Third Battalion's K Company. Rudy was thrilled that his mentor from Poston, Harry Madokoro, was also in K Company. He found the prospect of having Harry close by reassuring. His other buddy from Poston, Lloyd Onoye, was in I Company.

On the morning of May 1, a warm, breezy day on the Chesapeake Bay, the roughly forty-one hundred men and officers of the 442nd RCT filed up gangplanks onto gray-bellied Liberty ships. A brass band played, and Red Cross volunteers handed the men doughnuts and a form letter from President Roosevelt, telling them that they bore with them "the hope, the gratitude, the confidence, and the prayers of your family, your fellow citizens, and your President."[40]

Some of the men realized that it was Lei Day back home in Hawai'i. Ever since 1927, May 1st had been celebrated on the islands by the making and sharing of leis. With no flowers to be found on board, the boys from Hawai'i made off with crates of oranges from the galley, which they carefully peeled in long spirals. They hung the peels around each other's necks and around the necks of the mainlanders as well, wishing them and one another much aloha and feasting on the oranges.

At about the same time, on the other side of the Atlantic, the sun was setting over the horizon beside the once-lovely Italian seaside town of Anzio, thirty-one miles south of Rome. As the light faded, Nisei soldiers of the 100th Infantry Battalion crawled from foxholes and from bunkers in the rubble of what had until recently been people's homes.

They had not forgotten what day it was, either. Cautiously, they began to search for flowers, climbing over piles of masonry, circling ragged shell craters, trying to ignore the stench of the dead bodies buried under the ruins, as they collected the small, blood-red poppies of an Italian spring.

CHAPTER 14

THE LAW WASN'T YET FINISHED with Gordon Hirabayashi, nor was Gordon finished with the law. As the 442nd made its way across the Atlantic, he was waiting to be arrested again.

After he was released from the Catalina Federal Honor Camp in Tucson in December 1943, having served his ninety-day sentence, the government instructed him to report to the district attorney on his return to Spokane. Gordon decided he would ignore these instructions. As far as he knew, no other prisoner released from federal custody was required to report to a local DA. Once again, the requirement seemed to have been imposed on him solely because of his ancestry.

He went back to working with Esther and Floyd Schmoe, aiding displaced and incarcerated Japanese American families.

Then, in February 1944, he received a notification from the draft board in Seattle. After suspending the draft for Japanese Americans shortly after Pearl Harbor, the Selective Service had now decided to resume it.

Although Gordon, as a Quaker, was a conscientious objector, he, like all Nisei men of draft age, was sent a form titled "Statement of United States Citizens of Japanese Ancestry." The form required Gordon to disclose, among other things, any foreign languages he spoke, any clubs or associations he belonged to, his religion, and any magazines he subscribed to. It also required him to provide five references from people unrelated to him. Finally, it required him to declare his loyalty to the United States.

Gordon was deeply loyal to the United States and to its constitution. That's why he felt he had no other choice than to refuse to complete a form required only of Japanese Americans. He returned it to the draft board, pointing out that its very title made it discriminatory.

"This questionnaire, which I am returning to you unfilled, is an outright violation of both the Christian and the American principles of justice and democracy . . . The form is based purely on ancestry . . . I believe if I were to fill in this form I would be cooperating with a policy of race discrimination."[41]

To save everyone time, he included his address in Spokane so that they would know where to find him to arrest him.

Gordon was far from the only young Nisei man for whom the renewal of the draft and the required oaths of allegiance provoked a crisis of conscience. For hundreds, particularly those incarcerated in the camps, the questions again arose: Why should they be compelled to fight for a nation that removed them from their homes and denied them the rights and liberties afforded to other citizens? Why, if they were to serve, were they to be relegated to a segregated unit?

Most men in most of the camps complied with the orders to report. But others decided they would refuse to serve so long as their families were incarcerated. Thirty-two men refused at the Minidoka camp, thirty-one at Amache, five at Topaz, 106 at Poston, eighty-five at Heart Mountain, and twenty-seven at Tule Lake. Federal marshals descended on the camps and hauled the draft resisters off to local jails to await trial.

Before Gordon could be taken into custody again, there was something important he wanted to do first. He and Esther had decided to get married. On Saturday, July 29, 1944, with Gordon wearing a gray suit and a white carnation in his buttonhole and Esther in a simple white dress and holding an orchid corsage, they joined nearly two hundred of their friends, family members, and fellow Quakers in a church in Spokane.

After a period of silent worship, when Gordon and Esther felt the moment was right, they rose, held hands, put rings on each other's fingers, and declared their commitment to each other, to the Holy Spirit, and to the community assembled with them in the church.

ESTHER AND GORDON HIRABAYASHI'S WEDDING PHOTOGRAPH.

As they walked out of the church to have some photographs taken, a reporter approached them. This was something Gordon had been worried about. He had hoped to keep the wedding out of the news, but they had little choice but to answer the reporter's questions.

Esther asserted, as she had many times, that Gordon's race was irrelevant to her: "I love him . . . He is a sweet and loving character . . . Gordon is as American as I am." On Gordon's arrest and impending incarceration, she said, "He simply refused to fill out the form because it was sent only to Japanese-Americans and is discriminatory."[42]

The reporter seemed sympathetic, and his story cast the

news in a favorable light: "The barriers of race, national enmity, and criminal charges went down before love and Quaker brotherhood with the marriage here of an attractive young white girl to a Japanese-American youth."[43]

The news was also picked up by the Associated Press, and a shorter, sparer account, emphasizing that Esther was an "attractive white girl," spread quickly across the country and around the world. The story attracted wide attention, largely because in some states it was still illegal for people of different races to marry.

Within a few days, hate mail began to fill the newlyweds' mailbox. Most of the letters were anonymous, and most of the venom was directed at Esther, whom the writers repeatedly labeled a "traitor to her race."[44] There were crude drawings of Gordon with absurdly slanted eyes, a pernicious racial stereotype, accompanied by vicious racial slurs.

There were anonymous phone calls, too, always for Esther, voices hissing at her in the dark. Sometimes she argued with the callers, but usually she had to hang up on them and try to compose herself.

One letter of a very different sort arrived. It was addressed to both of them and was signed by the sender. It came from an American GI fighting the Japanese in the jungles of the Philippines. "I'm risking my life out here for the rights— you know, the values of our American citizenship and way of life. And that includes your safety and enjoyment. And I'm contributing this to your future." Enclosed was fifty dollars.[45]

Five months later, after spending Christmas with Esther—now newly pregnant with twins—Gordon was sent to federal prison at McNeil Island, Washington.

He was not the only Nisei confined at McNeil Island that December. Through the spring, summer, and fall of that year, nearly three hundred draft resisters from the camps had gone to trial in various federal courtrooms on charges of violating the Selective Service Act. Their trials unfolded in a number of different ways but concluded almost universally with convictions.

Sixty-three Nisei resisters from Heart Mountain were tried as a group. After addressing them in a dismissive and racist way as "you Jap boys" on the opening day of the trial and rejecting their constitutional arguments, Judge T. Blake Kennedy made short work of convicting all of them and sentencing them to three-year prison terms.[46]

And yet the point these young defendants were trying to make, about the fundamental injustice of their situation, did not go entirely unheeded. Many of the trials were held in communities in which the citizenry was overwhelmingly hostile to anyone of Japanese ancestry. One of these communities was the logging town of Eureka, in the redwoods of far northern California, where there was a long and often vicious history of anti-Asian sentiment. There, Judge Louis E. Goodman presided over the trial of twenty-seven Nisei draft resisters from the Tule Lake camp. Goodman was troubled by the notion of trying American citizens who had been transported to his courtroom from what he termed a "concentration center." How, he wondered, could they be considered free agents over their own affairs when their fundamental rights as citizens had been stripped from them?

Goodman waited until the last moments of the trial to reveal his thinking, but when he did, it was stinging: "It is shocking to the conscience that an American citizen be confined on the ground of disloyalty, and then, while so under duress and restraint, be compelled to serve in the armed forces, or be prosecuted for not yielding to such compulsion."[47]

With that, in front of a stunned courtroom, he dismissed all the charges. The Nisei resisters were free—but free only to return to the Tule Lake concentration camp.

CHAPTER 15

THE VESSELS CARRYING THE 442ND across the Atlantic and into the war joined a much larger convoy, and now more than ninety ships surrounded theirs, extending all the way to the horizon in every direction. Navy destroyers and cruisers on the convoy's flanks protected the ships from the German submarines they all knew might be lurking below the waves.

By day, porpoises cruised alongside. From time to time, whales surfaced, exhaling long, sonorous plumes of spray. Enormous jellyfish, white and pink, floated by. At night, the sea itself lit up as they slid over its surface, millions of phosphorescent organisms glowing green. It was, Fred Shiosaki thought, one of the most beautiful things he had ever seen.

By and large, the men weren't afraid. They didn't yet know enough to be afraid. But they had been away from home for a long time already. They yearned for the parents and siblings and friends they had left behind. At night, lying in their berths, they reached out and touched the things they had brought with them, things from home, things they hoped would carry them through the battles to come.

Some reached for crucifixes, some for small figures of the Buddha. Some had Bibles, some love letters from girlfriends back home. Some had rabbits' feet to bring good luck, some Saint Christopher medals for divine protection. Chaplain Hiro Higuchi had pictures of his wife, Hisako, his seven-year-old son, Peter, and Jane, the newborn daughter he had not yet met. One of the men in Kats's artillery unit, Roy Fujii, had a Honolulu bus token, which he wore on a chain around his neck. He planned to use it after the war to get from the docks in Honolulu back to his parents' house.

Sus Ito, another of Kats's artillery buddies, had a white senninbari his mother had sent him. Emblazoned with the image of a tiger—a symbol of safe homecoming—the traditional warrior's sash was embroidered with a thousand individual stitches, each made by a different woman with red silk thread to confer good luck, protection, and courage. Sus kept it folded up in his pocket, close to his heart.

Rudy Tokiwa also had received a gift from his mother. At Poston, Fusa had plucked a single grain of brown rice out of a hundred-pound sack of white rice. Somehow, it had survived the rice-polishing machinery. She sewed it into a pouch that Rudy now wore around his neck. When she sent it to him, she said, "This rice kernel was real lucky . . . It's the only one that lived through it and was able to keep this husk on.

So I'm sending you this so that you'll come home to us."[48]

Kats's 522nd Field Artillery Battalion docked in Brindisi—on the heel of the Italian boot—on May 28, 1944. From there, the men traveled by rail, in rickety cattle cars, northwest across Italy to rendezvous with the rest of the 442nd in Naples. The ride was slow and jolting, but, despite the discomfort, Kats was fascinated by his first glimpses of Europe. The scenery was lovely: gray-green olive trees, their trunks black and gnarled; sepia-colored hills; ancient villages perched on hilltops. It was hard to believe that this was a country at war.

But a few hours into the trip, when the train stopped in a bigger town and Kats climbed down from his boxcar to stretch his legs and look around, he found buildings crumpled by artillery fire and tanks, the rubble pushed into heaps by army bulldozers. Throngs of people—old men, women, and children—approached him, desperate, their hands outstretched, asking for food, for chocolate, for cigarettes, for help.

Worst of all was the children. Half-starved, they roamed the streets in small bands. Some wore cast-off German army jackets, others moth-eaten woolen trousers. Most were barefoot or wore tattered shoes.

When they saw Kats's American uniform, they ran up and clustered around him, their faces begrimed, their hair matted, their eyes hollow. They pleaded with him, calling him Joe, as they did every GI in Italy. He could not turn a street corner without encountering more of them.

He dug into his kit, pulled out his rations of chocolate and fig bars and cigarettes, and tossed them to the boys. But around the next street corner there were always more.

⋆ ⋆ ⋆ ⋆

WESTERN TUSCANY, 1944

On the other side of Italy, the main body of the 442nd arrived in Anzio, just south of Rome, and were landed by flat-bottomed landing craft onto the beachhead the Allies held there. Fred Shiosaki, weak from seasickness, walked down the ramp and glanced warily around him. Then he hoisted his gear and began marching with the rest of K Company through the shattered remains of Anzio's waterfront. The town was a hellish landscape of rubble, trenches, and barbed wire. Allied troops had been storming ashore here for five months under almost continual German fire. Only in the last few days had the Germans finally been driven back toward Rome.

Now the men of K Company arrived at their assigned area for making a camp, on a grassy, wildflower-strewn hillside five miles east of Anzio. Exhausted, and out of shape after nearly a month at sea, they threw down their gear, sat on the ground, and began picking through their K-ration boxes, trying to find something palatable to eat.

On the hike in, some of them had bartered with locals, exchanging cigarettes for bunches of sweet, white onions, baby carrots, and bags of string beans to supplement their rations.

While they were sitting in the afternoon sun, eating and looking out over Anzio and the turquoise sea beyond, news began to filter through. At the same time as they were boarding their landing craft the previous day, tens of thousands of men like them were pouring off similar craft in northern

France, in a place called Normandy, plunging into the cold Atlantic, wading ashore onto the beaches into gales of machine-gun and artillery fire. The much-anticipated Allied invasion of northern Europe had finally begun. The news about D-Day heartened the Nisei soldiers. Maybe this war they were about to become part of would be short and relatively easy.

Kats was chatting with George Oiye and Sus Ito nearby when one of their officers hurried up and told them to dig foxholes. Although the Germans were retreating north, they still had some very big guns within range. Suddenly, shells came screaming over their heads. To Kats, they sounded enormous, like washing machines hurtling through the sky. His stomach tightened. He dove for his foxhole. They all did. The barrage was short-lived, but when it was over and Kats climbed out of his foxhole, he noticed he'd gone weak in the knees with fear. The men dusted themselves off and laughed about what had happened. At least now they'd been under fire.

Then, as a full moon rose above the dark Italian hills, the black forms of German bombers appeared in the sky overhead. The Nisei soldiers dove for their foxholes and hunkered down again. The ground trembled with the concussions of bombs and occasionally a deeper roar and a more violent trembling when towers of flame and smoke rose from the munitions dumps down by the beach.

As soon as they realized they were not the target, the men peered over the edge of their burrows, scared but exhilarated too. The German planes finally peeled away and disappeared over the horizon, and the men crawled out of their foxholes again, talking excitedly, their hearts thumping.

The next afternoon, the men of the 442nd traveled to a new encampment, where they came across some old friends. For the Buddhaheads in particular, it was a joy to meet up with the men of the 100th Infantry Battalion. They sat in circles on the grass swapping news, talking story, showing one another photographs and letters from home.

It didn't take long for the 442nd men to see that these weren't the same guys they had known back home, nor were they the swaggering recruits with whom they had been briefly reunited at Camp Shelby. The men of the 100th had survived months of brutal fighting in southern Italy, and it had taken a toll on them.

Sometimes they looked off into space or got up and walked away in the middle of a conversation. They weren't unfriendly, but the new arrivals could see at a glance that there was something hardened about them now.

The next day, the 100th was formally attached to the 442nd RCT. In recognition of their extraordinary valor in southern Italy, the men of the 100th were allowed to keep their original designation and were called the 100th Infantry Battalion (Separate). Now, finally, the Nisei soldiers were all together, a single all–Japanese American fighting force.

Over the next two weeks, Nisei troops traveled north by truck, creeping toward the front lines and the German forces in western Tuscany. With each stop, their living conditions grew more spartan. There were no tents now. They slept in hay barns or under the stars. The civilians they encountered were, if anything, even poorer and more desperate here than those in Naples and Anzio. The faces of some were blackened with soot from living in caves, cooking over charcoal fires, eating whatever they could scavenge. And yet, as they passed some farmhouses—those that were still intact—Italians, mostly older people, ventured cautiously out to greet and encourage them.

As they approached the front lines, the terrain began to change too. The open coastal plain gave way first to rolling hills and then to forested ridges rising up toward mountain ranges. The Nisei troops began to see something most of them had never seen before: dead German soldiers, lying sprawled in fields or in ditches. The 442nd men stared silently at the corpses. The 100th guys didn't even seem to notice them.

On June 25, the men clambered out of their trucks and marched fifteen miles up narrow, winding roads into the hills. Shells whistled regularly over their heads now, fired from somewhere behind them—their own artillery pounding whatever it was that lay in the hills ahead.

When they encamped that night, Chaplains Yamada and Higuchi gathered as many of their men as they could, and they knelt together in the dirt and prayed. Whether they were religious or not, whether they were Buddhist or Christian or Shinto or none of the above, whether or not they had ever prayed in their lives, the men all prayed together now as the earth trembled and flashes of light lit up in the hills ahead. In the morning they were to attack.

Few of them slept, despite the long hike. They lay on the cold ground, looking up at the stars and wondering what battle would be like. But they couldn't know. They couldn't know that they were about to see and do things that would change them utterly. They couldn't yet understand that they were about to step off the edge of the world.

CHAPTER 16

—✕——✕——✕——✕——✕——✕——✕—

AT 6:22 ON THE MORNING of June 26, as the sun rose over western Tuscany, Cannoneer Roy Fujii picked up a shell to load into the breech of the howitzer Kats and his artillery crew had named Kuuipo—"Sweetheart" in Hawaiian. Kats crouched nearby, his fingers in his ears, having just set the coordinates for what was about to be the 522nd's first shot of the war. Their target was a formation of German vehicles about to get underway, two miles south of their position.

As Roy shoved the shell into the breech, it jammed. For a few moments, he wrestled with it. Swore at it. Wrestled with it some more. With the enemy vehicles liable to move at any moment, there was no time to lose. Roy picked up a sledge-hammer, and—disregarding the distinct possibility that he would detonate the thing and kill them all—began pounding on the shell.

At last it popped into the breech. One of the other men pulled the lanyard, the shot was off, and the 442nd's artillerymen were finally at war.

A little to the north, the young men of K Company were spread out, walking ten feet apart through fields and olive groves. They weren't sure where they were going except that it was somewhere in the hills ahead of them and that they should expect to run into German resistance by midmorning. Now and then they heard the sharp, splitting sound of a rooster crowing or the cooing of wood pigeons from dark forests of cork oaks.

But mostly the world was silent and still except for the shuffling of their boots, the clanking of their gear. Fred found to his surprise that he was not particularly afraid. More eager than afraid, anyway. Anxious for the fighting to start, if for no other reason than to know for sure that he wouldn't run.

Directly ahead of them on a low hill lay the town of Suvereto, an attractive jumble of buildings with red tile roofs. Beyond the town rose steeper hills clad in olive groves with vineyards on the lower slopes and mixed deciduous forests higher up. At the summit of those hills was a tiny hamlet called Belvedere that the Germans were using as an observation post from which to direct artillery fire on the countryside below.

The morning blossomed into a lovely early summer day, the kind when you could see for miles if you had a good vantage point. And that's exactly what the Germans had. All morning they had been biding their time, watching the Nisei advance on Suvereto. Now they unleashed a torrent of shrieking steel.

The worst of it fell on F Company. Mortar shells landed

among them with devastating effect, blowing men off their feet. Then Tiger tanks—enormous sixty-ton machines armed with massive eighty-eight-millimeter main guns and a pair of machine guns—rolled out from the cover of nearby woods and began to fire on the Nisei soldiers, more or less at point-blank range. Clutching their helmets to their heads, those F Company men who were still able to move scrambled and crawled for any cover they could find—a tree, a ditch, a stone wall, a ripple in the landscape.

In the midst of the chaos, Private Kiyoshi Muranaga grabbed a mortar tube, shoved some mortar shells into his pack, and scrambled out into the middle of a field. From there he had a clear line of sight on one of the tanks. His third shot landed directly in front of the tank but slightly short.

Before Muranaga could adjust the range and get off another shot, the German tank crew zeroed in on his position and fired, killing him instantly. But then, apparently rattled by the mortar fire, they withdrew into the woods, and Muranaga's squad was able to scramble to safer ground.

The K Company men were also in trouble. They were under direct fire from heavy machine guns immediately in front of them as well as from artillery pieces higher up in the hills. Fred and Rudy flung themselves on the ground and tried to dig in, frantically scraping the rocky, sunbaked earth with field shovels, bayonets, even their helmets.

By late morning, they had been pinned down for hours,

steadily taking casualties, unable either to advance on the town or to retreat to safer ground. Fred noticed that all the shells were coming from the Germans' side. Where was their artillery? Where was the 522nd?

After firing at the German vehicles, Kats and the rest of the 522nd had been ordered to move north to take up positions closer to Suvereto, where they would be better able to support the infantry. But all three batteries were still slowly wending their way up narrow country roads, largely unaware of the disaster unfolding in the hills.

By noon, Colonel Pence, Major General Charles Ryder, and Lieutenant Colonel Gordon Singles, commander of the 100th, had gathered enough information to come up with a plan for getting the 442nd out of its jam.

The commanders had held the more experienced Nisei soldiers of the 100th in reserve. Now orders went out, and within an hour A and B Companies of the 100th were racing uphill and circling around behind the Germans. Within another hour, they had silenced most of the German artillery, destroyed their observation posts, overrun Belvedere in house-to-house fighting, and sent the Germans fleeing on the road to the next town to the north, Sassetta.

The officers of the 100th had anticipated that retreat and had sent more men ahead to ambush the withdrawing Germans. They lay hidden in the dense foliage beside the road, clutching their guns, waiting for the Germans to rush into their trap.

They held their fire until all the German vehicles were nearly abreast of them, then they opened up with all they had, unleashing thundering volleys of fire.

It was more or less a massacre.

A few minutes later, more German troops rumbled down the road in trucks. As soon as their drivers realized they were driving into an ambush, they accelerated, swerving this way and that, trying to navigate their way around the abandoned vehicles littering the roadway.

The Nisei opened fire again. Men in gray uniforms tumbled from the backs of trucks and tried to run or crawl away.

Again, it was a massacre.

The 442nd's first day of combat had been brutal, its performance uneven at best. What started as a debacle for the Americans had turned into a rout of German troops—but only with help from the 100th, and only after the young men of the 442nd had seen things they'd never dreamed of seeing.

Rudy Tokiwa found a patch of ground to stretch out on. Even though the evening was chilly, he was sweating. And he felt sick. Sicker than he'd ever felt. So did Fred. A shaken Hiro Higuchi wrote to his wife about his first experience of war: "It's just hell—un-dreamable goriness and death . . . Someday I will tell you all about it, but now I don't want to think about it."[49]

★ ★ ★ ★

Over the last days of June and into July and then August, the 442nd fought almost continuously, day and night. Along with other elements of the Fifth Army, the men crept north through western Tuscany, mile by mile, sometimes yard by yard, trying to push the well-dug-in Germans north toward the Arno River.

As the terrain grew even steeper, the Nisei soldiers had to crawl uphill, grabbing at roots and rocks. In the humid heat of an Italian summer, it would have been grueling work even without someone shooting at them.

The 442nd and the 100th continued to take tremendous casualties. By early July, nearly four hundred of the roughly four thousand Nisei troops who arrived in Anzio in May had been killed or wounded.

But every time one of them went down, the others learned something new about surviving. Never linger in a crossroads— German artillery will have it zeroed in. Never pause in the shade under a single tree in the middle of an open field, for the same reason. And never, ever, kick a can in the road.

One thing the Germans had learned about American boys was that if they came across a can lying on the ground, they were almost certain to kick it down the road. In Italy, it was likely to be sitting on a land mine.

Indeed, most of the casualties were from mines. The Germans laid thousands of them across the Italian countryside, and they were nearly impossible to detect unless you got down on your hands and knees and crawled, inspecting the ground in front of you. Even then you could easily fail to see them and wind up losing an arm, a leg, or your life.

In the early hours of August 25, Harry Madokoro—Rudy's friend from Poston, one of those who had talked the others into signing up—stepped on a mine. In an instant, he simply disappeared in a shower of mud, metal, blood, and bone. There was nothing Rudy or any of his friends could do but stare silently at the crumpled form lying in the dark void where Harry had once been.

★ ★ ★ ★

As a runner, Rudy was particularly wary of mines. He spent much of his time out on his own, carrying messages to and from the front lines. He was tired and dirty all the time. His feet ached. His face was unshaven and perpetually caked in sweat and dust. His uniform was torn and ragged, and it stank. At night he sometimes had to crawl into culverts or bushes alongside some dried-up stream, alone and unfed, to try to get some sleep.

But because Rudy was Rudy, he found opportunities wherever he went. When passing through villages, rather than using the streets, he hopped fences from one backyard to the next. The backyards were where the good stuff was: a head of cauliflower, a handful of green onions, a nice fat cabbage, a fistful of baby carrots, half a dozen eggs—or, better yet, the hen sitting on the eggs. When he could, he left the owner a bar of chocolate or a pack of cigarettes as payment for whatever he took. When he couldn't, he declared the booty the spoils of war.

He foraged in the open countryside too, collecting sweet, plump wild figs from the woods and harvesting watercress growing by the sides of ponds. Sometimes he came across rabbits, but he always passed them by. As a kid in Salinas, he had a pet rabbit that followed him around the farm and snuggled with him at night. He couldn't bring himself to kill a rabbit.

Rudy seldom returned without a pack full of fresh food for his guys in K Company, and he made a lot of friends that way. The Buddhaheads were particularly grateful. Sometimes they would just prepare okazu—little side dishes of vegetables to go with their rations. When they had enough to work with, they made chicken hekka, a Hawaiian stew.

As they spooned it into their mouths from their stainless-steel mess kits, they smiled, often for the first time in days, even though the artillery boomed and machine guns rattled in the hills around them. It was the taste of home.

★ ★ ★ ★

After months of nearly constant combat, the 442nd finally got a break. The men headed south to the seaside village of Vada. If there was a place in Italy that looked like Hawai'i, this was it—a mile-long stretch of white-sand beach. There were even palm trees scattered along the shoreline. The Buddhaheads lost no time making WAIKĪKĪ BEACH signs and affixing them to the palms. Then they waded eagerly into the warm aquamarine water and swam.

Fred Shiosaki and some of the K Company men commandeered a skiff, rowed a safe distance from the swimmers, and threw hand grenades into the water. As white columns of water erupted from the surface, a bounty of seafood floated up: sea bass, octopus, sea bream, squid—all stunned by the explosion, easy to grab, and ready to grill or to slice up for sashimi.

The Nisei soldiers spent long days on the beach, feasting on fish and cooking up Hawaiian dishes like chicken hekka and kālua pig, reading novels, playing their guitars and ukuleles, talking story—all of them, Buddhaheads and kotonks, speaking mostly Hawaiian Pidgin now. They tried desperately to push out of their minds what they had just been through.

Many of the officers stayed with Italian families, sharing their meals and drinking good wine with them. Chaplain Yamada was with a family of professional entertainers. When they found out he was from Hawai'i, they pulled out some cellophane grass skirts and began to perform one of their regular acts, shimmying and swaying a sort of hula—much to Yamada's thigh-slapping delight.

Yamada and Higuchi spent most of their time sitting together in a favorite haystack, watching Italian farmers thresh wheat and working on their correspondence. Balancing typewriters on their laps, the two chaplains labored over condolence letters to the families of men who had been killed during the preceding few weeks.

The soldiers of the 442nd were not the same men who had landed in Italy four months before. They had come anxious to prove their loyalty, determined not to bring shame on themselves or their families. They were united by their shared ethnic identity, by friendships developed on the beaches in Hawai'i or in the mud at Camp Shelby. But now there was something more uniting them. Now they were bound together by something born out of their experience in battle, by the certain knowledge that before this war was over more of them would die, and that it was up to each of them to watch out for the others.

★ ★ ★ ★

News of Harry Madokoro's death in combat had reached the Poston concentration camp, where a memorial service was quickly arranged. As the last desert twilight faded away and a few bats flitted through the purple sky, someone helped Harry's sixty-six-year-old mother, Netsu, onto the stage at the Cottonwood Bowl. Originally just a circle of dust scraped out of the sagebrush, the Cottonwood Bowl had become one of the most pleasant places in Poston. With a stage built of timber and stucco in the style of a Japanese theater and situated in the cooling shadow of several large cottonwood trees, it was a place where people could come together for community events.

Over the past two years it had been the site of theater performances, graduation ceremonies, Christmas pageants, band concerts, variety shows, and other community gatherings.

Lately, though, it had been used more and more often for memorial services for fallen Nisei soldiers.

SERVICE FOR FALLEN COMRADES IN ITALY.

As Mrs. Madokoro sat watching somberly, a bugler summoned a color guard. The camp's Boy Scout troop led a salute to the American flag. Priests from all three of the camp's churches gave readings from Buddhist and Christian texts.

Friends approached Mrs. Madokoro and laid flowers at her feet and read her telegrams sent from Harry's friends. A choir sang. The camp's military police fired a salute with their rifles. Finally, the bugler played taps. As the last long, sad, lingering notes drifted out beyond the circle of lights, into the absolute darkness of a desert night, friends helped Mrs. Madokoro back to her quarters, room 13-G in Block 213 in the Poston concentration camp.

CHAPTER 17

✕ ✕ ✕ ✕ ✕ ✕ ✕

OVER THE SUMMER, THE 442ND'S reputation spread far and wide. Fighting their way up the western coast of Italy, the men had taken one hilltop town after another, gaining valuable ground for the US Army. They had taken heavy casualties, but their battle record was outstanding. The Germans came to respect and fear the Nisei soldiers, whom they called "the little iron men." American newspapers and newsreels brought their accomplishments into movie theaters from Maine to Honolulu, and accounts of their exploits appeared in the military newspaper, *The Stars and Stripes*, drawing the attention of other American servicemen around the world.

Suddenly the Nisei soldiers were in high demand. General Mark Clark wanted to keep them in Italy with his Fifth Army. But General Alexander Patch wanted them in his Seventh Army in France, and Patch was backed by General George S. Patton and General Dwight D. Eisenhower, the supreme commander of Allied troops.

So the men of the 442nd boarded Liberty ships again, this

RUDY TOKIWA BRINGING IN CAPTURED GERMAN SOLDIERS IN ITALY.

time bound for Marseille. Their numbers were boosted by 672 replacement Nisei troops newly arrived from the States.

By October 13, all three battalions of the 442nd had arrived in France at an assembly point roughly forty miles west of the German border. There they were formally attached to the Seventh Army's 36th Infantry Division under the command of General John E. Dahlquist.

The 36th was composed mostly, though not entirely, of men from Texas. Now they and the Nisei soldiers stood together facing the Vosges—the region of heavily forested mountains that lay between them and Nazi Germany.

Studded with medieval castles, the Vosges was a dark and forbidding place. Armies had clashed there since well before ancient Roman times. When Kats, Fred, Rudy, and the other Nisei soldiers contemplated what new horrors might lie

THE 442ND GOING INTO BATTLE IN THE VOSGES.

in store for them in those forests, their stomachs tightened. They knew now what combat was like, and they dreaded it.

At 3:15 a.m. on October 14, Kats and his gun crew slipped a round into Kuuipo and fired the first shot of the new campaign. They settled into firing almost continuously through the night, pounding the dark mountains and softening up the German defenses.

With the 522nd's guns rumbling behind them and white flashes lighting up the gray underbellies of the clouds ahead, the men of the 442nd began slogging through muddy fields of wheat stubble and trudging down wet country roads. Their objective was to secure the high ground around the town of Bruyères, where several roads and a railway line converged.

The Germans threw everything they had at the approaching Americans, contesting every yard of territory with mortars and shells, streams of machine-gun fire, and snipers on hilltops and in church spires.

Over the next three days, the four thousand residents of the town huddled in their basements while the Nisei soldiers fought furiously for every yard they could gain from the Germans.

Just before dawn on the morning of October 18, K Company exited the woods and entered the flatter, more open terrain immediately in front of Bruyères. Suddenly engulfed by the roar of battle, Fred stumbled over muddy furrows, bullets whipping by on both sides. Shells whistled over his head. Columns of black earth and fractured yellow stone erupted in front of him and behind him. Searing hot shards of shrapnel flew in all directions, making weird fluttering sounds. The smell of explosives and diesel fuel and mud and blood filled the air.

Closing in on the town, Fred and the men near him dropped to the ground and began to crawl forward on their bellies as streams of machine-gun fire poured from the windows of nearby farmhouses and machine-gun nests hidden behind stone garden walls. They returned fire, lobbed mortars at the buildings, threw hand grenades at each machine-gun nest in turn, and, when it was silenced, moved on to the next.

When K Company reached the town, the men advanced cautiously, running in a crouch from one doorway to the next.

Lobbing grenades, kicking down doors, racing to rooftops, clearing houses, the Nisei gradually drove the Germans out of Bruyères. By early evening, most of the town was theirs.

German shells and mortar rounds continued to fall in the streets as a furious battle for the high ground to the east raged on. The streets were littered with slate roof tiles, bricks, piles of stone and mortar, and burned-out vehicles. Here and there a dead German in a bloodied uniform lay in the street. The smell of gunpowder lingered in the air, and the whiff of death.

Then Fred noticed flags emerging from upstairs windows—French flags and the Croix de Lorraine, the emblem of the Resistance, French citizens who had fought against Nazi rule. The townspeople poured out into the rainy and rubble-strewn streets. At first, confused by seeing Asian people, they exclaimed, "Chinois?! Chinois!"

The Nisei, pointing to their uniforms, tried to explain. "No, no, Americans. Japanese Americans!"

"Japonais?!" The French looked at one another, clearly baffled. Japan was supposed to be the enemy.

But nobody really cared what the Nisei soldiers looked like. Young women, old men, children, all ran to them, embraced them, and kissed them on both cheeks. Old men brought out bottles of wine and strings of sausages and patted their liberators on the back. Children flocked around them cheering, shouting, "Merci, merci, merci!" Thank you, thank you.

Fred dug out a chocolate bar from his kit, broke it into bits, and handed the pieces out to the kids. Then he moved on.

Over the next few days, K Company inched deeper into the mountains. At night, the men hunkered down and tried to catch some sleep, sliding into trenches the Germans had dug or craters left by their own artillery shells. The holes were half-full of rainwater, but the men were beyond caring. They just lay against muddy walls, closed their eyes, and let their feet and legs soak. A few chose to lie out in the open instead, despite the risk of shells.

Fred lay in one of the trenches, his eyeglasses smeared with mud, teeth chattering. His feet ached terribly, and he pulled off one of his boots and a soggy sock to have a look. The foot was an odd shade of purple—a sign of trench foot, the slow, agonizing death of the nerves and tissues.

When morning came, gray and wet and cold, they got up and pushed on to the northeast. For two more days and two more nights, they kept moving forward, yard by yard, under almost continuous fire, with nothing to eat but cold K-rations, nowhere to sleep but in the mud.

By late October 24, they had taken control of the villages of Belmont and Biffontaine and pushed the Germans deeper into the Vosges.

One day, Rudy was making his way back to the battalion's command post to report on the successful completion of a maneuver when K Company's medic, James Okubo, stopped him.

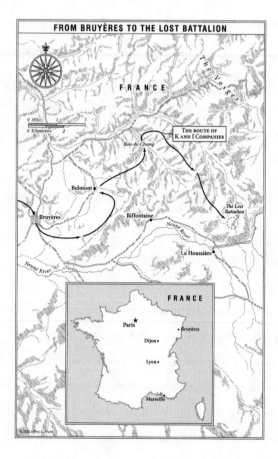

"When you came through, did you see any dead Germans out there?"

"Yeah."

"You see any of 'em alive?"

Rudy shrugged. "I don't know. I never look."

Okubo had been up all night tending to the wounded, but he wanted to see if there were wounded Germans still out on the field. "I can't carry a rifle. Will you go with me?"

Rudy shrugged again but picked up a Thompson submachine gun and led Okubo into the hills.

The two men began to sort through a pile of German dead and eventually found one boy who was still alive. Okubo patched him up as best he could, and the two of them carried him back to an American aid station.

There, Okubo turned to Rudy and said, "I hope you don't get mad at me now." Rudy replied that he was glad they'd helped the boy. But the truth was, it seemed odd to him, after he and his guys had spent so much time trying to kill Germans, to be trying to save one.

It wasn't really that he objected. He just didn't particularly care one way or another. But it got him thinking.

I wonder, he thought. *When I get out of this—if I do— whether I'll still be a human being.*[50]

★ ★ ★ ★

K Company had now been on the battlefield for seven days and nights. Some units had been out eight days. Finally, two Texas units—the 141st and 143rd Infantry Regiments— began moving up through the 442nd's lines to relieve them.

Fred and Rudy and the rest of K Company, their uniforms stiff with caked mud, stumbled out of the mountains into the shattered remains of the village of Belmont. There they collapsed in whatever shelter they could find—anywhere with a dry corner or a pile of hay or even just a cold slate floor to stretch out on—and fell asleep.

CHAPTER 18

— ✕ — ✕ — ✕ — ✕ — ✕ — ✕ — ✕ —

A LITTLE MORE THAN FORTY-EIGHT hours later, at 3:00
a.m. on October 27, Fred was sleeping soundly on the floor
of a tavern when Rudy shook him awake.

Fred fumbled for his eyeglasses. "Hey! What the hell?
Why you wakin' me up?"

"No argue. Just get your gear . . . We're moving back up."[51]

All around him, other K Company guys were grumbling
in the dark, groping for rifles and helmets, pulling on wet
boots, stuffing their gear into packs.

An hour later, they shuffled out onto wet cobbled streets.
It looked to Fred as if both the Third Battalion and the 100th
were assembling, with K and I Companies out front, taking
the lead. Behind them, he could hear tanks starting to move,
and more men marching. Whatever this was about, it was big.

Up in the mountains, where the rain was threatening to
turn to snow, more than two hundred men were trapped behind enemy lines, desperately trying to stay alive.

Four days before, on October 23, General Dahlquist had

ordered some of the 141st Infantry Regiment of his Texas Division to push along a series of ridges north of Biffontaine. At first, the Texans met only light resistance, and, as evening approached, all was surprisingly calm.

Which didn't make any sense.

Then, as darkness fell, the forest behind them erupted with gunfire. The men hastily set up a perimeter defense and dug in for the night.

In the morning, some of them tried to retrace their steps and came under heavy fire. Those who survived stumbled back into camp to report that the Germans had built a blockade on the road during the night.

There was no doubting it now. The Texans had been lured into a trap. Stuck at the end of a ridge, on a mountaintop behind enemy lines, they were sitting ducks, under nearly continuous artillery fire and repeated ground attacks.

For the next several days, by radio, General Dahlquist repeatedly ordered the stranded men to fight their way out. When those attempts failed, he ordered other companies from the 141st to relieve them, all to no avail.

Finally, growing increasingly desperate, he gave the order to wake up the battle-weary men of the 442nd and send them up the mountain. If none of his regular guys could get the Texans out, maybe the Nisei could.

Nobody had told Fred Shiosaki or anyone in his squad about any trapped Texans. As dawn approached, and the patches of sky above the trees shifted from absolute black to slate gray, he heard the sound of a battle up ahead—the rattle of machine guns, the cracking of rifles, the concussions of grenades, the growling of tanks.

He still had no idea where they were going, what their objective was, or what they were up against. All he knew was that they had come to an abrupt halt and their officers were suddenly screaming at them to spread out and take cover.

Kneeling behind a tree with a rifle in his hands and a mortar tube strapped on his back, Fred tried to make sense of the situation. The sounds of battle extended off to both the left and right of him. Judging from the amount of fire coming at them, there seemed to be a sizable enemy force somewhere ahead in the wet gray murk.

ADVANCING TOWARD THE LOST BATTALION IN THE VOSGES.

K Company started to advance. Fred tried to move up, tree by tree, toward the still mostly invisible Germans ahead as periodic bursts of machine-gun fire ripped through the forest around him. Dirt and stones and bits of bark flew in all directions.

Then 105-millimeter howitzer shells began to whistle overhead. George Oiye and Sus Ito had crept out in advance of the line. Using a forested ravine for concealment, they'd spotted some German tanks about a hundred yards in front of K Company and called in their coordinates.

Kats Miho and the 522nd guys began firing on the reported position of the tanks. However, because the terrain was so steep, they were having a hard time with accuracy, and the barrage had little effect on the tanks. By early afternoon, K and I Companies had advanced only a matter of yards in the face of the relentless tanks and machine-gun fire. Roughly three miles away, the surrounded Texans were almost entirely out of rations, completely out of medical supplies, and fast running out of hope.

At about 3:30 p.m., the Germans launched a full-scale counterattack. Fred and his squad frantically dug in wherever they happened to be.

Then someone shouted, "Tank! Tank!" A German Panzer IV tank rumbled out of the foggy woods ahead of them, firing point-blank into K Company's positions.

Shells slammed into stout trees, shattering their trunks,

KATS MIHO FIRING A HOWITZER AT A HIGH ANGLE IN FRANCE.

toppling them over on men on the ground. Alongside and behind the tank, German infantrymen advanced steadily, firing machine guns. Within minutes they were within fifty yards of the shallow depression where Fred lay.

It was clear that the enemy was about to overwhelm them.

Out of the corner of his eye, Fred saw a friend, Matsuichi Yogi, stand up, a bazooka up on his shoulder, and run full tilt toward the tank.

Fred sucked in some cold, wet air and held his breath.

Right in front of the tank, out in the wide open, Yogi stopped and knelt. With bullets whistling all around him, he fired and scored a direct hit. Flames erupted from the underside of the tank, black smoke poured out of its hatch, and it ground to a dead stop.

By the time Yogi made it back to K Company's lines, the German attack was tapering off. The gray-uniformed enemy was ghosting back into the foggy twilight.

Exhausted as they all were, nobody in the 442nd slept much that night. Nobody said much either. There really wasn't much to say. When the sun came up, more of them were going to die, and they all knew it.

So they tried to imagine they were somewhere else. Home, maybe. A warm bedroom. With family laughing downstairs. Pots and pans rattling in the kitchen. The smell of ginger being grated, tea being brewed, bread being toasted. Anywhere but here. Any time but now.

When dawn came, the Nisei continued to push toward the stranded Texans. The only realistic option for reaching them was down the middle of a narrow ridge, through a series of heavily fortified positions while under constant fire.

All morning, General Dahlquist bellowed orders over the radio, demanding to know why progress was so slow, why they weren't breaking through to his Texans.

Colonel Pence decided to go up to the front line to check on the situation for himself. Almost as soon as he arrived, his jeep came under attack. He suffered severe leg wounds and had to be hastily evacuated from the battlefield.

For the men of K Company who witnessed the incident, it was tough to see Pence go down.

It fell now to their other commanding officer, Lieutenant Colonel Alfred A. Pursall, to make Dahlquist understand the near impossibility of what he was asking for.

Pursall decided that he, too, needed to see the situation on the ground. He asked Rudy to go with him. It wasn't the first time Pursall had sought out Rudy for a dangerous mission. He respected the younger man's judgment, particularly in tough situations.

With automatic fire ripping through the trees above them, Pursall and Rudy worked their way forward a few dozen yards, out past the line, crawling uphill on their bellies through wet moss and rotting leaves to get a better view of what was throwing so much fire at them.

What they saw was chilling.

The entire hillside above them bristled with German machine-gun nests and dug-in infantry armed with heavy weapons. Higher upslope, they could hear tanks and half-tracks moving.

Pursall asked Rudy what he thought about trying to take the hill.

Rudy answered as he always did, honestly and bluntly. It would be insane. They needed to wait, to bring up more firepower first.

Pursall nodded.

But by the time they worked their way back downslope, General Dahlquist himself had appeared on the scene. The general looked around and saw exactly what he didn't want to see: men dug in on all sides.

"I want you guys to charge," he yelled. "Charge, charge, charge!"[52]

Pursall planted himself squarely in front of the general, standing closer than was comfortable for either man. Speaking slowly but firmly, he tried to explain the situation. That a charge now would be suicidal. That they needed to bring other units up first.

Dahlquist, red in the face now, didn't want to hear it.

Finally, Pursall wheeled around and said to Rudy, "Okay, let's go."

Rudy hesitated. The last thing he wanted was to start back up that hill again. "Where're we going, sir?"

"We've got to take the general up, to show him what we are up against."

Rudy and Pursall began leading Dahlquist uphill. Bullets snapped into trees all around them. Rudy was horrified, but he wasn't going to be the first to dive for cover, so he kept walking.

Pursall pointed out the German positions to Dahlquist—all in all, an impenetrable wall of resistance.

Dahlquist seemed unimpressed.

Rudy couldn't believe what he was seeing: two senior officers standing in full view of the Germans, nose to nose in the pouring rain, arguing with each other as bullets whipped by.

Eventually, Dahlquist spat at Pursall, "I'm ordering you, you will attack! That's an order!"

Pursall grabbed Dahlquist by the lapels of his shirt: "Those are my boys you're trying to kill. Nobody kills my boys like that. Nobody."

The two men stood for a long moment, seething at each other. Then, Dahlquist wheeled around and walked away, shouting over his shoulder, "That's an order!"

Pursall stared grimly up the hill in front of him. Then he pulled a pearl-handled pistol from a holster, stood up, and yelled, "Come on, you guys! Let's go! Let's go!" He started up the hill, firing the pistol, and bellowing again, "Let's go! Artillery, too! You charge, too!"[53]

Chester Tanaka looked up, saw Pursall, and thought, *My God! If he is going to walk up into that fire, I guess we'd better, too.*[54] He stood up and motioned for his men to follow him.

Fred Shiosaki stared at Pursall for a moment, disbelieving. Then, like Tanaka, he rose to his feet and started hobbling forward, his swollen feet throbbing with pain.

George Oiye heard someone next to him clicking his bayonet onto his rifle. To his right, his radioman, Yuki Minaga, got up and took a few steps forward. Even though he was scared to death and armed with only a pistol, Oiye got up and started running up the hill, too.

So did Sus Ito.

So did Rudy.

CHARGING UPHILL INTO ENEMY FIRE IN THE VOSGES.

They all did. With their fathers' words echoing in their minds, their mothers' love beating in their hearts, one by one, then as one, the men of K Company rose and began to charge up the hill, shooting blind through the tangle of trees looming above them.

Down the line, in I Company, Private Barney Hajiro saw K Company go. He stood and began moving steadily uphill, spraying the terrain ahead of him with automatic fire.

The rest of I Company rose and followed him. Sergeant Joe Shimamura yelled, "Make! Make! Make!"—"death" in Hawaiian.[55] Others roared insults in Japanese or Hawaiian Pidgin, hurling them at the Germans. Most of them just gritted their teeth and ran, slipping and sliding in the mud, tripping over roots, getting up and running again, expecting to die at any moment.

A torrent of steel and lead descended on them. Mortar shells plunged down among them. Machine-gun fire ripped them apart as they ran. A bullet smacked into the head of the man running next to Fred. Howling eighty-eight-millimeter tank shells slammed into trees, shattering them, toppling them over onto the men.

A shell exploded a few yards in front of George Oiye. The blast blew him thirty feet downhill and deafened him. He staggered back onto his feet and started up the hill again. Another shell hit a tree next to him and fell right at his feet, spinning in the mud, but didn't go off. He stepped over it and kept going.

Yet another shell slammed into a tree directly ahead of Fred. This one did explode, and something hard and hot sliced into Fred's side. *God, I'm hit*, he thought as he went down.[56]

He rolled onto his back, pulled up his shirt, and found a jagged piece of steel shrapnel embedded in his abdomen. But there wasn't much blood.

K Company's medic, James Okubo, crawled over to him, pulled the shrapnel out, bandaged the wound, and told Fred he was okay, to get up and keep going. He did.

The higher they climbed, the steeper the slope became. Grabbing at tree roots and rocks, they hoisted themselves higher, drawing closer to the German tanks, which were pointing directly downhill, firing point-blank at them. Dust and smoke mixed with the fog in a dense yellow-gray soup that made it hard to discern friend from foe. The men crawled over logs, stepped over dead bodies, hurled grenades uphill.

And kept going.

Then, suddenly, just as Fred reached the top, the sounds of battle simply ceased. One moment there were explosions and shrieks and wailing and bellowing, the next near silence. Nothing but the crack of occasional rifle shots, the whumping of artillery off in the distance, and the moaning of wounded men. In the woods ahead of him, Fred saw something he had never seen before: Germans running away from him.

"My God," he muttered to himself. "It's done."

Then he looked around and thought, *But there's hardly anybody left.*[57]

Of the hundreds of men who had started up the mountain three days before, fewer than two dozen in K Company were still alive and able to walk. In I Company, there were even fewer.

CHAPTER 19

—✕——✕——✕——✕——✕——✕——✕—

AT DAYLIGHT, THE REMAINS OF K Company moved forward again. All the company's commissioned officers were now dead or wounded, so command fell to Sergeant Chester Tanaka.

When artillery and mortar shells rained down on the Nisei soldiers once more, it was clear that the Germans had regrouped in the forest ahead of them. K Company dug in about four hundred yards from the top of the ridge where the Texans were trapped. The Germans, meanwhile, were charging the Texans from all directions, closing to within thirty yards in a matter of minutes. It seemed clear that their intent was to kill them all before the Nisei could reach them.

The encircled Texans threw everything they had left at the Germans, hurling grenades and unleashing furious automatic weapons fire. But they knew they wouldn't be able to sustain it for long. Soon they'd run out of ammunition and would be at the mercy of the Germans. And there was no reason to believe the Germans would have any mercy to show them.

Then, in the midst of the chaos—mingled with the smells of high explosives, shattered wood, and mud—the Nisei and the Texans began to smell smoke. A few minutes later, they saw billows of white smoke rising from the German-held valley beyond the ridge.

As the smoke screen spread out, filtering through the trees, the Germans pulled back off the ridge and simply disappeared.

A patrol from I Company had been advancing cautiously, on hands and knees much of the time, ahead of the main force. One of their number, Mutt Sakumoto, saw a pale face peering around a tree. The face disappeared, then reappeared, then disappeared again.

Eventually, a figure stepped cautiously out from behind the tree, clutching a rifle and staring hard at the approaching Nisei. Finally, the soldier threw down his rifle and ran downhill, shouting, whooping, laughing. When the two came face-to-face, technical sergeant Edward Guy of the 141st Infantry Regiment embraced Sakumoto of the 442nd in a bear hug.

At about the same moment, Rudy Tokiwa and Chester Tanaka, approaching from a different direction, saw a helmet moving in a foxhole. They froze. Tanaka leveled his rifle, preparing to shoot, but hesitated. It was an American helmet. Tanaka lowered the rifle, and Sergeant Bill Hull scrambled out of the hole.

Someone unseen in the woods called out, "Hey, the 442 guys are here!" Texans began rising out of the earth, emerging from camouflaged foxholes all around the Nisei soldiers like prairie dogs popping from their burrows, their faces gaunt, begrimed, their eyes hollow.

Realizing that their ordeal was finally over, they hugged one another, some of them laughing, some blinking away tears. When Rudy approached them, one of the Texans croaked out, "God, thank you, thank you, thank you."[58]

As the Texans filtered out of the woods and onto a muddy logging road, a newsreel cameraman arrived by jeep and began to film the scene. The rescued GIs shook the Nisei soldiers' hands and patted them on their backs. The Nisei handed them cigarettes, candy bars, and canteens full of water. The Texans smiled wearily and said thank you again but then walked quickly on. None of them wanted to linger. They just wanted to get off the mountain.

★ ★ ★ ★

On November 9, in Parker, Arizona, a little town just north of Poston, Private Raymond Matsuda wandered into a barbershop to get a haircut. He was on crutches, having been shot in the knee in Italy that July. Recently released from a hospital in California, he was on his way to visit friends incarcerated in the Poston camp.

Raymond figured he should get spruced up before heading to the camp. So, wearing a uniform emblazoned with the 442nd patch and six or seven other army ribbons and badges, including the Purple Heart, he hobbled through the barbershop's double swinging doors.

He did not see, or he chose to ignore, a sign on the door. JAPS KEEP OUT, YOU RATS.

The proprietor, Andy Hale, took one look at Matsuda, strode over to him, cussing, and shoved him back out through the doors, crutches and all.

Asked about it later, Hale was unapologetic. "I don't want none of their business . . . I sure as hell won't work on a Jap." When someone pointed out that Matsuda was both an American citizen and a wounded US Army soldier, Hale just snarled, "They all look alike to me."[59]

At Poston, every morning since Rudy's departure for the army, before the dawn began to lighten the desert sky, before the doves began to coo in the mesquite trees down by the river, his mother, Fusa Tokiwa, was one of the first to rise. She checked her slippers carefully to make sure no scorpions had moved in during the night. Then she stepped quietly out of her room and made her way through the chill desert air to the women's showers. When she got there, she turned the cold water tap on and stepped into the freezing stream, gasping and shutting her eyes tight against the pain. As she endured the intense physical discomfort, she prayed silently for her son, that God would let her sacrifice be enough, that he would allow Rudy to come home safe.

On November 11, the camp newspaper, the *Poston Chronicle*, reprinted parts of an Associated Press story, the first brief telling of what had happened in the Vosges. The article quoted one of the rescued Texans, Private Walter Yattaw, expressing his gratitude. "It really was ironical that we were so glad to see the Japanese, but boy, they are real Americans."

The piece had few specific details about what Fusa Tokiwa and everyone in camp most wanted to know: the casualties. That news would soon begin to arrive in dribs and drabs, brought by blunt telegrams or by military officers arriving unexpectedly in full dress uniforms.

****

After a further week of fighting and a few days' rest, the surviving members of the 442nd assembled on November 12 in a snowy field so General Dahlquist could formally acknowledge their role in rescuing what by now everyone was calling the "Lost Battalion."

Fred Shiosaki stood with what was left of K Company, his rifle over his shoulder, watching wearily as Dahlquist and a cluster of officers approached them in a jeep.

Like all the men around him, Fred was tired in his bones and tired in his soul. His face was pinched and pale, his cheeks devoid of their usual rosiness. His eyes were downcast, blank. A dusting of snow clung to his shoulders and sleeves, and his feet still throbbed from the ravages of trench foot.

At last, the ceremony got underway. A color guard paraded past the Nisei, led by the 442nd's regimental band. Dahlquist and Lieutenant Colonel Virgil Miller clambered out of their jeep. Miller had taken over command of the 442nd when Pence was wounded.

Now he and Dahlquist stepped forward. Instead of addressing the men, Dahlquist paused, looked at the paltry number of men lined up in front of him, a fraction of what he had expected, and scowled. He turned to Miller and snarled, "Colonel, I told you to have the whole regiment out here. When I order everyone to pass in review, I mean *everybody* will pass in review!"[60]

STUNNED SURVIVORS OF THE LOST BATTALION RESCUE STANDING IN REVIEW FOR GENERAL DAHLQUIST.

Miller's jaw clenched, and a long, awkward silence ensued. Then he pivoted slowly, looked the general in the eye, and, his voice wavering, croaked, "General, this *is* the regiment. This is all I have left." His eyes were filled with tears.[61]

Dahlquist fell silent. For the first time, he realized the price the Nisei had paid to rescue the Texans. Far more Nisei had been lost than Texans had been rescued. He stuttered out a few words of congratulations then silently made his way down the lines of soldiers, pinning on the chest of each a ribbon representing a Distinguished Unit Citation.

As he passed and shook their hands, the men simply stared past him, looking over his shoulder at the dark mountains beyond.

CHAPTER 20

—✕——✕——✕——✕——✕——✕——✕—

NEARLY NINE HUNDRED OF POSTON'S young people were now in the armed services, and even as the casualty lists from France grew, more were signing up. Almost every week, friends and well-wishers gathered for farewell ceremonies at the Cottonwood Bowl. The new recruits left with a particular sense of pride. After three years, in spite of the heat, the dust storms, the monotony of mess-hall meals, and the degradation of confinement, the people at Poston, as at the other camps, had created extraordinary communities behind barbed wire, and they were justly proud of them. In the face of injustice and humiliation, they had stood tall. They nourished their spiritual lives, educated their children, found a refuge in creativity and productivity.

They dug irrigation canals from the Colorado River to the camp, and land that had been nothing but sagebrush and sand was now green. Vegetable patches flourished; tea gardens surrounded ponds full of koi and goldfish. Carefully transplanted cottonwood trees offered at least a bit of shade over barracks and walkways.

Some people wrote haiku and practiced calligraphy, or they carved ironwood and polished semiprecious stones into exquisite sculptures. Others crafted paper flowers from pages torn from mail-order catalogs and tissue wrappers from oranges and apples and used the paper flowers to create ikebana arrangements, adding seedpods, vines, and twigs they found in the surrounding desert.

The Cottonwood Bowl now hosted almost daily theatrical performances, ranging from kindergarten pageants to formal Kabuki productions. It continued to be used for memorial services, too, of which there were ever more as the 442nd's casualties mounted.

Buddhist priests and Christian ministers tended to their flocks. Doctors, lawyers, architects, farmers, carpenters, truck drivers, florists, and electricians all brought their specialized skills to bear on improving the quality of camp life.

There were still many hardships and difficulties, though, and many disruptions to traditional family life. Young people now preferred to take their meals with their friends and not with their families. Those who had grown up on remote farms, observing their parents' traditional ways, now mixed with young people who had grown up wearing the latest fashions and listening to the latest popular music.

Some young Japanese American women, flying in the

face of traditional gender norms, were determined to serve in the military. In February 1943, shortly after Nisei men were first allowed to serve, the Army Nurse Corps began accepting Japanese American women. Then, in September, the Women's Army Corps also began to enlist Japanese American women.

For the most part, the women found themselves doing clerical work, acting as typists, stenographers, and supply clerks. But forty-eight of them who had good Japanese-language skills were assigned to the army's Military Intelligence Service Language School, to work as translators of intercepted Japanese communications.

Another 350 joined the Cadet Nurse Corps, a nonmilitary program designed to replace the thousands of nurses who left American hospitals to serve overseas. The program offered a rare opportunity for Japanese American women to pursue a career outside the home.

Many of the Nisei women who wanted to serve faced strong opposition from friends and family members. Those who persisted were largely motivated by the same reasons that had led Nisei men in the camps to enlist.

Some had brothers in the army and wanted to support them. Some wanted to get out from behind the barbed wire of the camps. Some saw an opportunity to acquire job skills they could use after the war. Most, though, simply wanted to show their loyalty to their country, to do what they could to serve it, and to help end the war as quickly as possible so they could all return home. For many, though, that dream was cut short when they found that accredited nursing programs more often than not refused to admit Japanese American students, on the basis of their race.

Then, on December 17, 1944, a front-page article in the *Poston Chronicle* sent shock waves through the camp. For months, the government had been quietly wrestling with whether to do away with the exclusion zone, close the camps, and end the incarcerations.

Secretary of the Interior Harold Ickes and First Lady Eleanor Roosevelt had been urging the president to agree to a plan for resettling the "evacuees," as the government called them, back on the West Coast. Even the army had concluded that there was no military necessity for keeping people in the camps. Through the summer and early fall, with his campaign for reelection underway, President Roosevelt was wary of giving the impression that he was easy on the Nisei and their parents. Three days after his reelection, however, he relented.

And now the news was out. In just weeks, most people of Japanese ancestry would be allowed to travel and live anywhere in the United States, including on the Pacific coast.

At Poston, as at all the camps, the news was met with a profound sense of relief mixed with an equally profound sense of anxiety. What might happen to them when they tried to return home? Would they even have homes to return to? Already there were disturbing reports of early returners being met by violence. Despite not knowing what they might face, the inhabitants of Poston began to leave, making their way back across the country, with no ceremony marking the end of their unjustified incarceration.

CHAPTER 21

BY THE TIME THEY CAME down out of the Vosges, the Nisei soldiers were broken in every way that war can break young men. Between May 1943 and November 1944, they had taken 790 casualties—most while rescuing just over two hundred members of the Texas unit. They needed rest. To grieve for lost friends. To come to terms with what they had been through.

They boarded trucks and headed south to take up defensive positions on the French-Italian border. Their official mission was to block the Germans crossing from northern Italy into France, but nobody expected the Germans to make such a move, so there was little chance they would see significant combat.

The army's intention was to give the Nisei a break, and for many it came just in time. From the Maritime Alps above Nice and Monaco, they had stunning views of a bright-blue Mediterranean Sea and coastline. At sunset, they watched the sea turn purple and the sky blossom orange and violet.

They felt safer than they had in a long while, and they slept as they had not slept in months.

They spent their free time roaming up and down the sun-drenched French Riviera, sitting at sidewalk cafés and eating in restaurants with white-linen tablecloths. Kats had his photograph taken in a studio that catered mostly to celebrities and movie stars. Rudy and some friends explored the luxurious bars and high-stakes casinos in Monte Carlo. Fred picked plump oranges from trees overhanging shady lanes.

They all sat in darkened movie theaters, watching American-made films with French subtitles. And, suddenly, to their surprise, they were watching themselves. French movie theaters had begun showing newsreels featuring the rescue of the Lost Battalion. The Nisei were fast becoming celebrities in France. At each showing, the audiences burst into applause then patted the men on the back and shook their hands as they filed out of the theaters.

When on duty, the soldiers spent much of their time on reconnaissance patrols, climbing up and down rocky hillsides or huddled with radios and binoculars in natural caves and concrete fortifications studying German movements across the border in Italy.

Occasionally, Nisei patrols wearing white parkas ran into similarly clad German patrols, and fierce firefights erupted on snowy, windswept mountainsides. Now and then artillery duels broke out, with hundreds of shells flying in both directions. In January alone, six Nisei soldiers were killed and twenty-four were wounded.

Even when up in the mountains, they contrived simple pleasures, staging epic snowball fights and strumming ukuleles as they sat around campfires. Kats cut an oil drum in half, filled it with steaming-hot water heated over a fire, and used it as an ofuro. There he would sit for hours on end, happily soaking in the tub while looking over the blue Mediterranean spread out below him.

By the end of February, it was clear that what they were calling the "Champagne Campaign" was about to end. Sooner or later, they were going to have to go back into heavy combat. They dreaded it. A year before, they couldn't wait to get into the war. Now they just wanted to go home.

The artillerymen of the 522nd learned that they were to be detached from the 442nd and sent back north to eastern France to join in the final assault on Nazi Germany. Kats, like Sus Ito and George Oiye and most of his artillery buddies, hated to leave this place of relative ease and his many infantry friends. But orders were orders. They packed up their gear and headed north.

A curious air of secrecy hung over infantry's future. Some feared they would be sent to the South Pacific to enter the war against Japan. A few dared to think they might be going home. Most resigned themselves to uncertainty.

On March 17, they boarded trucks bound for Marseille.

It was a lovely spring morning, and they were determined to extract the last ounce of pleasure from their Riviera sojourn. As many of them as could fit climbed onto the roofs of the trucks, and they sat dangling their legs over the edges, strumming guitars and ukuleles, throwing lemon drops to children running alongside.

The mood changed abruptly when they arrived at the waterfront, where enormous gray landing craft awaited them. They were told to strip all unit-identifying marks from their uniforms and equipment. Whatever lay in store for them, the army didn't want the world to know about it.

General Clark had been impressed when the 442nd fought for him in Italy the previous year. He'd told Pence then, "The courage and determination which the men of the 442nd RCT have displayed during their short time in combat is an inspiration to all."[62] In the seven months since, especially after learning of their exploits in the Vosges, Clark had been lobbying hard to get the Nisei back.

Throughout the fall and winter of 1944, the Allies had hurled themselves repeatedly at a line of German fortifications stretching all the way across Italy, from north of Pisa in the west to the Adriatic Sea in the east. But they had made little headway. As long as the Germans remained entrenched in their mountain caves and concrete bunkers, the Fifth Army was stuck.

Clark wanted to send the Nisei troops against them.

And he wanted their presence in Italy to be a surprise to the Germans, who he knew feared them.

He did not expect the 442nd to break through the line. Nobody had been able to do that. But if they pressed hard enough and fought as hard as they had in the Vosges, the Germans would have to shift troops to the west, and that would greatly aid the larger Allied effort.

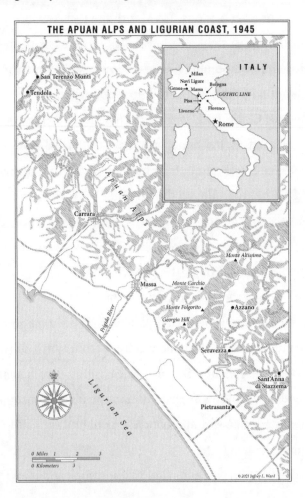

Neither Fred nor Rudy nor any of the 442nd's men knew this when they disembarked from their landing craft in the war-ravaged harbor of Livorno in northwestern Italy. All they knew was that they were back in Italy and heading back into combat somewhere up in the mountains.

Over the next several days and nights, they hid in barns by day and traveled in the backs of trucks with blacked-out headlights at night. When they reached the beautiful little town of Pietrasanta, they continued by foot. Fred and Rudy hoisted their gear and fell into a column of K Company men shuffling up a narrow road.

The guys in the 100th headed off in a different direction, disappearing in the darkness.

Someone hissed that the road might be mined and to stay off to one side or the other.

As the road steepened, Fred began to struggle, huffing and puffing, his legs aching. It had been months since they'd been on a real march like this, and he was out of shape.

A little before 4:00 a.m., after five hours of trudging uphill, they arrived in a darkened village called Azzano in the Apuan Alps. The officers quietly rapped on the doors, waking up the villagers, informing them that they had houseguests and telling them to keep their lights turned off.

In small groups, the Nisei soldiers shuffled silently into cellars, barns, and kitchens—anywhere they could be kept out of sight. Sprawled out in hay and on earthen floors, they tried to get some sleep.

In the morning, the villagers offered their guests whatever food they could find in their meager pantries—eggs and cheese and olives, and something the men would remember for the rest of their lives: pancakes made from freshly milled chestnut flour, drizzled with mountain honey.

All day, the Nisei stayed out of sight, knowing that German observers in the surrounding mountains would be keeping an eye on the village. Just before midnight, they tied their dog tags together so they wouldn't make any sound and rubbed soot on their faces. I and L Companies slipped quietly out into the main street and followed a dark path through the forest into the narrow valley below.

As they crossed a river at the bottom of the valley, they were spotted by two German snipers. A brief firefight erupted, and the Germans were quickly dispatched. Walking single file, each man holding on to the pack of the man in front, they followed an Italian partisan up a steep and rocky footpath on the other side of the valley.

Their mission was audacious: to make what seemed an impossible climb up the nearly vertical mountainside, surprise the Germans from behind, and capture the high ground before morning revealed their presence to enemy observers on nearby peaks.

Well before dawn, after climbing nearly three thousand

feet, the first of the soldiers crawled out onto a narrow saddle of land running between the summits of two peaks. With their officers whispering commands, the companies then split into two, each group scrambling across rock ledges to approach one of the two mountain peaks.

L Company came across a cave with unmanned machine guns at its mouth. The guns were pointed at the route they had just safely traveled in the dark.

Private Arthur Yamashita fired a burst from his automatic rifle at the entrance of the cave, and after a few tense minutes seven sleepy Germans crawled out, waving strips of white cloth to signal their surrender.

The gunfire had alerted German sentries in distant observation posts, and now enemy artillery opened fire. The Americans responded with their own artillery fire, and soon the mountains were thundering.

But by the time the sun rose, at 8:00 a.m., the battle for the high ground had been won, and the 442nd had forced open a crack in the Germans' mountain defenses.

At about the same time as the first Nisei troops reached the top of the mountain from the east, the 100th Battalion attacked from the southwest. As they approached the German perimeter, Company A blundered into a minefield. When the first mine exploded, the men, many of them recent replacement troops, scattered, promptly detonating seven more mines and killing many.

The Germans, alerted by the explosions and the screaming, began raking the confused mass of men with machine-gun fire and tossing down clusters of grenades. Seeing a disaster in the making, some of Company A's more experienced men ran forward, plunging into the melee.

One of those more experienced men was Rudy's close buddy, Sadao Munemori. With his men in disarray and bullets whistling past him in the dark, he rallied his men and led them through the minefield, quickly closing to within thirty yards of several entrenched machine-gun nests.

As they neared the German gunners, his men dove for cover behind rocks and in shallow shell craters, but Munemori charged directly at the Germans, hurling grenades and taking out two of the nests. Then, under heavy direct fire, he headed back toward his men. He had nearly made it to the crater where two of his men—Akira Shishido and Jimi Oda—were sheltering when an unexploded grenade bounced off his helmet and rolled toward them. Without hesitating, Munemori dove for the grenade and smothered it with his upper body just as it exploded, killing him instantly but sparing the lives of Shishido and Oda.

On the other side of the mountain, it was K Company's turn. Following in the footsteps of I and L Companies, Fred and Rudy worked their way down to the river in the valley. The sun was well up now, and the enemy could see their every move.

A squad of Germans concealed in a nearby marble quarry unleashed a barrage of mortars at them, pounding the area with mortar rounds like hailstones in a thunderstorm. There was no place to hide and no place to run. All the men could do was dig in and call for artillery strikes on the marble quarry and the German guns.

Some of the newer, less experienced troops did try to run, leaping to their feet and sprinting upstream or downstream, stumbling over the stones in the river. Fred bellowed at them—"Get down! Get down!"—but panic had set in. Confused, the new men ran directly into a maelstrom of flying shrapnel and shattered stone. Within minutes, three were dead and twenty-three wounded.

Fred, Rudy, and the other surviving members of K Company knew they had to get out of there. Retreat wasn't an option. The only way lay directly ahead. They rushed forward and began to scale the mountain, hand over foot.

Over the next forty hours, the Nisei fought among the mountain peaks day and night. The operation cost thirty-two Nisei soldiers their lives, with dozens more wounded. But in a little less than two days, the 442nd did what nobody had thought possible. The men opened a gaping hole in the western end of the German defenses. The Allied armies now had a clear route north, and the German army in Italy was all but doomed.

As they withdrew, the Germans continued to rain down

shells, and the Americans' artillerymen pounded them in return. Somewhere between the two, Rudy Tokiwa got caught in the cross fire. Whether it was a German shell or an American round that fell short he never knew, but Rudy was too close when it hit. A dozen jagged pieces of hot shrapnel sliced into his lower body. The wounds weren't mortal, but they were crippling. For Rudy, the war was over.

CHAPTER 22

— ✖ — ✖ — ✖ — ✖ — ✖ — ✖ — ✖ —

FAR TO THE NORTH, NEAR midnight on the cold, rainy night of March 12, the 522nd Field Artillery Battalion crossed the Saar River and entered Nazi Germany. Attached now to the 63rd Infantry Division in General Patch's Seventh Army, the Nisei artillerymen met no opposition. By 11:30 the next morning, they had dug in on German soil for the first time and begun firing on targets to the east.

From the moment he entered Germany, Kats was perplexed by what he saw. A few years earlier, this would have seemed a lovely place, the Germany he had read about since childhood. A land of fairy tales, with castles on hilltops, tidy villages, and whitewashed cottages.

But in March 1945, it was hard to see any loveliness in the German countryside. It wasn't just the buildings crumpled by Allied bombing, the burned-out wreckage of German tanks and half-tracks strewn alongside the roadways, the black pillars of smoke rising from the remains of factories and railroad depots.

It was more a general sense that something dreadful lay in the land's immediate past or immediate future—he couldn't be sure which. Kats could see it in the eyes of the civilians they passed, standing in barn doors, peering out from behind shutters as the Nisei rumbled through villages in their trucks.

He had seen war-shocked civilians in Italy and France, but this was different. The faces he saw seemed to suggest that something beyond even the horrors of war, something profoundly dark, lay just over the horizon ahead of them.

Kats and his crew fell into a regular routine, setting up and firing their guns for a few hours then moving on. When their scouts found pockets of German resistance, the 522nd pounded them into submission before tanks and infantry filled in behind to mop up. By mid-April they were pursuing a German army in full collapse.

Whenever they had a break, Kats and his buddy Flint Yonashiro foraged for food, scouring the countryside for chickens and vegetables to supplement their K-rations—as they had done in Italy and France.

On one occasion, they returned with more than twenty squawking chickens stuffed into sacks and served up a barbecue for all the men in their unit. But the biggest prize was when they stumbled across an abandoned warehouse stacked to the rafters with enormous wheels of Dutch cheese, crates of canned Portuguese sardines, cases of schnapps and cognac, and boxes of cigars.

There were even some brand-new accordions still in their boxes.

Whenever they had some downtime, the men feasted on their bounty, passing around bottles of schnapps, slicing up wedges of cheese, and making hilarious attempts to play Hawaiian music on the accordions.

But the breaks were few and far between, and a cold reality was always just around the next bend in the road. And that reality was increasingly difficult to grasp.

Kats struggled to process all that he was seeing. A whole town reduced to rubble by Allied bombing. The bodies of German soldiers dangling from lampposts, hanged by their Nazi officers for desertion or cowardice. Dead horses sprawled in front of artillery pieces, as if this were a nineteenth-century war.

Then, on April 29, US troops approached the Dachau concentration camp in southern Bavaria, where tens of thousands of Jews, Poles, Russians, and other groups oppressed by the Nazis were incarcerated, treated brutally, and used as slave labor. Outside the camp, they found thirty-nine boxcars filled with 2,310 corpses. The bodies of men, women, children, and babies were all heaped together in a macabre tangle of limbs. The stench was overwhelming.

Inside the camp, thousands of starving prisoners in striped uniforms—victims of the Nazis' relentless racist agenda of destroying Jews and other ethnic minorities—gathered. As their numbers increased, they pushed at the gate, threatening to overwhelm and stampede their liberators.

THE "CORRIDOR OF DEATH" IN SOUTHERN BAVARIA, 1945

An SS officer, Untersturmführer Heinrich Wicker, came forward to negotiate the surrender of the camp. The Americans weren't interested in negotiating anything. They marched Wicker to the train full of corpses and demanded answers.

As they moved deeper into the camp, the GIs' anger mounted. Piles of naked dead bodies stacked up outside a building like firewood. A mountain of shoes—many of them children's shoes. Some kind of interrogation room, its concrete walls splattered with blood.

Gaunt, hollow-eyed people rushed up to the GIs, cheering, embracing them, dropping to their knees and embracing their legs. Others, too weak to walk, crawled out of the barracks on hands and knees. Some stayed inside, lying in their own filth on wooden bunks, more dead than alive. They stared at the GIs with eyes behind which no one now lived.

In Dachau's empty coal yard, a few GIs—by now in a cold and furious rage—lined up Nazi prison guards against a wall and shot them, killing several dozen, perhaps more, before a senior officer found them and put a stop to it.

In other parts of the camp, prisoners took matters into their own hands, beating an unknown number of guards to death. Untersturmführer Wicker was never again seen alive.

There is no firm evidence that any of the 522nd participated in the initial liberation of the main camp at Dachau, but by late afternoon at least a few Nisei soldiers had entered the camp.

Toshio Nishizawa recalled driving through the open gates and being shocked by what he saw. Josef Erbs, an eighteen-year-old Romanian Jew, remembered lying sprawled on the ground when a Japanese American soldier bent over, picked him up, and carried him to an aid station. It was the first time Erbs had seen an Asian person of any sort. He took note of the shoulder patch on the man's uniform: blue, with a white hand holding a torch—the insignia of the 442nd RCT.

What the Nisei soldiers saw at Dachau was just one part of a network of Nazi concentration camps. Some were slave-labor camps like Dachau. Others, like Auschwitz-Birkenau, were devoted to the systematic murder of millions of Jews, Poles, Romani, disabled people, LGBTQ people, and anybody else that the Nazis labeled as undesirable. The next day, April 30, Adolf Hitler died by suicide in a bunker in Berlin.

That same morning, the main column of the 522nd moved south again, breaking down gates and liberating prisoners from some of the subcamps surrounding Dachau. On the road, they came across scores more bodies splayed out in muddy fields, ditches, and pinewoods.

The corpses were dressed in the same thin, striped uniforms as the prisoners at Dachau, and many of them had gunshot wounds to the backs of their heads—victims of a forced march out of the camp and execution when they couldn't keep up.

On May 2, Kats and George Oiye, along with some other

Nisei artillerymen, found scattered lumps in the snow. When they brushed the snow from the lumps, they found what they feared they would: more bodies.

Then, nearby, they noticed a boy crouching in the snow.

Solly Ganor, a Lithuanian Jew, one of those thousands marched out of Dachau days before, had awoken that morning covered by snow and surrounded by bodies. Now he watched warily as men in uniforms approached him.

It must be his turn to be shot.

He resigned himself to his fate and waited for the bullet.

Then he realized the men were speaking English. He looked up and saw Asian men smiling down at him. This did not make sense to him. He wondered if he were dead and these were angels. One of the angels hovering above him said, "You are free, boy."

Ganor grappled for the English word. "Who?" he finally croaked out.

"Hey! He speaks English."

"Americans," one of the men said. "Japanese Americans."[63]

One of the angels handed him a chocolate bar. Ganor took it but set it aside. He would not eat the chocolate. That would be like eating a treasure. "You would not eat the *Mona Lisa*,"[64] he would later say.

CHAPTER 23

AT 2:41 ON THE MORNING of May 7, 1945, Colonel General Alfred Jodl of the German armed forces met US Army Lieutenant General Walter Bedell Smith at a schoolhouse in Reims, France, and surrendered. The Third Reich was defeated, and the war in Europe at an end.

When the news was announced in Great Britain, tens of thousands poured into London's Trafalgar Square and Piccadilly Circus, cheering and hugging each other. In Paris, throngs of French civilians mingled with American and British soldiers around the Arc de Triomphe, singing the French national anthem, "La Marseillaise," and dancing down the Champs-Élysées.

News of the surrender arrived in the United States just in time for the evening editions of the newspapers. Millions read the Associated Press's lede: "The greatest war in history ended today with the unconditional surrender of Germany."[65]

Perhaps half a million jubilant people jammed into New York's Times Square. Blizzards of torn paper and confetti drifted down from tall buildings at Rockefeller Center and on Wall Street. In the Garment District, workers ripped open bales of fabric and threw thousands of yards of rayon, silk, and wool from the windows, draping passing cars in colorful cloth.

In most of the country, though, the response was more muted. Here and there, church bells rang, and people gathered to offer up prayers of thanksgiving. Americans turned on their radios, called loved ones, and congregated on front lawns to talk over the news.

They all knew the war in the Pacific was not yet over. This was not what they had been waiting for since Pearl Harbor.

In Italy, Chaplain Higuchi was the first member of the 442nd's Second Battalion to hear the news. He asked for permission to address the men and let them know.

The men were puzzled. It was odd for the chaplain to address them all together on any day other than Sunday.

Higuchi mounted a platform and started by asking the men to sing "America." He led them through the first few familiar lines: "My country, 'tis of thee, / Sweet land of liberty, / Of thee I sing." Then he told them, "Fellas, the war in which all our friends who slept with us and ate and died and wanted to see this day . . . the war is over."[66]

No one cheered. A soft sigh rippled through the ranks, but nothing more.

Higuchi looked out at the upturned faces and saw tears

running down cheeks. He knew what he was looking at. He felt it himself. He asked them to take a minute for silent prayer, to thank God for their deliverance, and, more than that, to think of the men who were not there, who had died to make this day possible, and to think also of the folks at home who would never see their sons and husbands and brothers return.

A few of the men shouted and threw their hats in the air, but only a handful, and they were new replacement troops, the ones who had not seen any fighting, who had not lost any friends, who had not seen young bodies torn open.

The rest of the men went back to their assigned tasks. They were happy it was over, but grim-faced. Nobody got out ukuleles. Nobody danced hula.

Fred Shiosaki couldn't manage to get too worked up about the news. Too much had happened. Too many friends were gone. Too many bloody dreams haunted him at night. He thought, *Jeez. Well, I made it. I think I made it.*[67]

Then he took a nap.

For Fred, and for most of the Nisei soldiers, the end of the war in Europe was clouded not only by their grief and sheer exhaustion but also by the realization that the moment they were waiting for was still off in the future.

Nobody could say how long the waiting would go on. That would be decided in the Pacific. The same Associated Press story that announced the German surrender had stated it starkly with a single line printed in boldface, WAR ON JAPS CONTINUES.

★ ★ ★ ★

Several months later, in Japan, on the other side of the war-torn world, Kats's sister Fumiye Miho was waiting impatiently for the next train into Hiroshima. It was a warm, humid morning, August 6, 1945, and she was going to be late for work.

In the past few months, life had only gotten harder for Fumiye, her sister, and their family—as it had for everyone in Japan. In March, they had barely survived yet another firebombing of Tokyo by the Americans, so her brother-in-law packed up all his dental equipment and moved them to a village fifteen miles outside the city of Hiroshima—the same village from which Katsuichi and Ayano Miho had emigrated to Hawai'i thirty-four years before.

There they lived in a Buddhist temple with four other refugee families. Their living spaces were separated by curtains, and the only water available had to be carried uphill in buckets from a dirty stream. Fumiye's brother-in-law had already fallen ill from drinking the water. Her sister Tsukie's two children were perpetually sick and hungry, and there was little food to be had except for potatoes and parsnips.

The only saving grace was that Fumiye had a job in the city center of Hiroshima, translating English news broadcasts for the Japanese government.

And today she was late.

As she approached the ticket booth to inquire about the next train into Hiroshima, a flash of light unlike any light Fumiye had ever seen nearly blinded her. Everything turned white, almost translucent, just for a moment, before the normal yellow light of a summer morning flickered back on.

The world went suddenly silent.

Fumiye turned in the direction from which the white light had come. A long, low rumbling arose in the distance, growing louder and louder until it became a sustained roar. The ground seemed to quiver. Then the gray morning sky over Hiroshima resolved itself into a towering, tulip-shaped cloud, vaguely violet in color, that rose higher and higher in the sky before darkening and flattening out into something vaguely like a mushroom.

By that afternoon, word had reached the village that the whole of central Hiroshima had been destroyed after a single American warplane appeared over the city.

The village authorities commanded everyone to return to the railway station at 5:00 p.m. to help with the wounded being evacuated from the city center.

Many of the area's schoolchildren had gone into the city to do community service work that day, so the platform was packed with anxious parents when Fumiye arrived. When the first train evacuating the wounded from the city pulled in, a long wailing arose from the crowd. Almost none of the parents could recognize the blackened, disfigured children who stumbled off the train or were carried off on stretchers.

The next day, Fumiye took a train to within two miles of Hiroshima and then walked the rest of the way. Even before she got into the flat, empty wasteland where the city center had been, she could smell the overwhelming stench of burned flesh and see black columns of smoke rising from the ashes.

For a week, she walked through the ruins, helping the survivors in any way she could, sleeping at night on the charred lawns of what had been city parks. She tried to ease the dying of an old woman who had turned purple and blue from what Fumiye would only later learn was radiation poisoning.

Fumiye herself was fortunate enough to experience only mild effects from her exposure to radiation in Hiroshima. After the war, she was reunited with Kats and the rest of her family in Hawai'i. The experience of witnessing the suffering of so many people following the bombing of Hiroshima turned her into a lifelong pacifist. She became a Quaker and spent the rest of her life traveling the world preaching peace and compassion.

Sixty-six thousand people died at Hiroshima. Another sixty-nine thousand were injured. On the morning of August 9, three days later, the United States dropped a second bomb on the town of Nagasaki. Another thirty-nine thousand people were killed and twenty-five thousand injured there.

CHAPTER 24

ON THE SAME MORNING THAT Nagasaki was bombed, the SS *Waterbury Victory* pulled up to Pier 40 in Honolulu Harbor, carrying the first 241 men and officers of the 442nd RCT to return to Hawai'i.

Young women came on board and handed out doughnuts and pineapple juice. They were followed by dancers in grass skirts, who wore plumeria and hibiscus flowers in their hair. The dancers hung leis around the necks of grinning soldiers dressed in crisp khaki uniforms with arrays of medals and decorations on their chests.

Then the women danced hula, swaying on the foredeck as the men pulled out guitars and ukuleles and sang the familiar songs of home that had sustained them throughout the ordeal.

After some speechifying by local officials, Lieutenant Colonel Pursall led the men down the gangway to a motorcade that whisked them away to the stately grounds of 'Iolani Palace, where thousands of people were waiting for them: their parents, siblings, buddies, girlfriends.

A HULA DANCER WELCOMES A VETERAN HOME
ABOARD THE SS *WATERBURY VICTORY*.

They showered the men with more leis, and with kisses and embraces.

Then, at last, they sat under the familiar banyan trees on green grass and ate kālua pork and laulau as the fairy terns again circled above them in graceful white loops against a blue Hawaiian sky.

In the wake of the bombings of Nagasaki and Hiroshima, news swept around the world that Japan had surrendered on August 14. Now, finally, Americans were able to celebrate as never before in the history of the nation. In New York, the largest crowd the city had ever seen poured into Times

Square. Men climbed lampposts waving American flags. In Seattle, sirens wailed and car horns honked as people streamed out of offices and storefronts into the streets. In New Orleans and Boston and Chicago and Los Angeles, in every city, midsized town, and tiny hamlet in America, it was the same: an outpouring of unrestrained relief and joy.

★ ★ ★ ★

In Europe, many of the soldiers of the 442nd had to wait for weeks or months before they could return to the United States.

Fred Shiosaki got the nod to head for home in late October and made his way back to Spokane, Washington. When he walked into the warm, familiar, steamy smells of the Hillyard Laundry, his whole family was waiting there to greet him. His older brother, Roy, had just returned from serving in Europe, too.

Fred's mother and sister, gleeful and laughing, embraced him, and his father shook his hand. Then he looked him in the eye and simply said, "You did well."[68] After that, he went to the front of the laundry and took down the two blue stars hanging in the window.

★ ★ ★ ★

Rudy Tokiwa was still hobbling on crutches from his injuries when he left Italy for home. And, like so many soldiers, not all his wounds were physical. When he was passing through Chicago on his way west, a car backfired, and Rudy and another GI nearby hit the ground. When Rudy got up and dusted himself off, he realized, for the first time, that it might take him a while to get over the war—both physically and mentally.

When he arrived back at Fort Douglas, Rudy learned that the Poston camp had been closed. No one could tell him anything about his parents and sister or about or any of the people who had been incarcerated there. It was as if they had all just disappeared. Concerned and frustrated, he decided to head for the place his father had always talked about settling: San Jose, California.

In the bus station in San Jose, there was a Red Cross stand, set up to aid returning GIs. Rudy explained to the woman working there that he had just come back from overseas and that the camp his parents had been incarcerated in was now closed. He wondered if she could help him.

The woman looked up and studied Rudy a moment. "There's a place on Fifth Street. A bunch of Japs are livin' there."

A sailor waiting in line behind Rudy pushed forward. "Are you calling this man a 'Jap'? Do you see his ribbons? He fought overseas! Who do you think you are?"

The sailor put Rudy in a cab that took him to the Buddhist church on Fifth Street. And there, sure enough, Rudy found his parents.

His mother leaped up and wrapped her arms around him when he limped into the room. His father remained seated, looking him over, and then said simply, "I'm very glad to see you home. Are your wounds bad?"[69]

Rudy assured him he would be okay.

Although he made no mention of it that day, pinned to Rudy's chest, along with a Purple Heart and a Combat Infantry Badge, was a Bronze Star. Before he left Italy, the army had awarded him the medal, in front of fifteen thousand GIs and a number of colonels and generals.

Rudy had felt embarrassed standing on a platform as soldiers marched past, saluting him. But something had surged in him, something that was not there when he left Poston three years before. He had been angry then—angry at the country that incarcerated his family, that humiliated his parents, that cost them their farm and their livelihoods.

In many ways, he was still angry and would stay that way for a long time. But standing there with the medal on his chest and a brass band playing behind him, with the 442nd colors and the American flag fluttering in the breeze, he had a moment of peace and pride that he would remember for the rest of his life.

You know, he thought, *it doesn't make no difference what you look like. It's what you're doing and what you've done for the country that counts.*[70]

★★★★

It was December 1945 before Kats Miho was finally able to begin the journey home to Hawai'i. As the boat approached Oʻahu and rounded Diamond Head, Kats and nearly all of the 232 servicemen aboard crowded the rails. A nearly full moon hung low over the sea to the west, and all of them wanted to catch that first glimpse of the Aloha Tower and the white sands of Waikīkī in the moonlight.

There were no hula dancers to greet them. Sailors and soldiers had been returning to Hawaiʻi for so many months now that only a few newspaper photographers bothered to show up. Roy Fujii took the Honolulu bus token off the chain around his neck, gave Kats a wave, climbed on a bus, and headed for his parents' home up in the hills.

Kats looked around for his own parents. And there they were, waiting and waving.

The war years had been hard on the Miho family. Ayano had had no choice but to sell the hotel on Maui. Katsuichi had just been released from imprisonment. The two of them were scraping out a living picking macadamia nuts for a commercial farm on Oʻahu—just as Katsuichi had done decades before when they first arrived in Hawaiʻi.

It was going to take a lot to put their lives back together. For now, though, Kats savored the moment. Just being with his parents, luxuriating in the warm tropical breeze, smelling the sea, and seeing the morning mist clinging to the green-humped mountains above the city was enough.

CHAPTER 25

—✕—✕—✕—✕—✕—✕—✕—

EVEN AFTER ALL THE CASUALTIES the Nisei soldiers suffered in World War II, it would take decades for Japanese Americans to fully win their rightful place in American society. Millions of employers still refused to hire them, and the jobs that were available to them were mostly low paying and menial. Racist slurs and insults still met them everywhere they went. They were still excluded from owning property in certain neighborhoods. At the end of the day, they were still "Japs" to many of their compatriots.

And all the medals and honors earned by their sons and brothers in the war did little to alleviate the trauma that thousands of mothers and fathers, sisters and brothers experienced in the camps—or when they tried to return home. Thieves had looted possessions left in storage. Vandals had shattered nursery greenhouses, destroyed merchandise, spray-painted threats on their property—*Japs Keep Out!* Squatters had occupied homes and refused to leave.

A tough road lay ahead for most Japanese Americans—

civilians and veterans alike—before the country's leadership formally recognized and addressed the wrong that was done to them.

But very slowly a start was made, particularly among those aware of what the Nisei soldiers had accomplished. President Harry Truman pushed for a restoration of property and civil

LIEUTENANT COLONEL PURSALL AND PRESIDENT TRUMAN REVIEWING THE 442ND, WASHINGTON, DC, JULY 15, 1946.

rights for Japanese Americans, and he strove to gain greater public recognition for what the 442nd had done.

In 1952, Japanese immigrants were finally allowed to apply for citizenship. Fred and his siblings coached Kisaburo and Tori, quizzing them on civics and American history for their citizenship exams.

When they both became American citizens, it was a moment of profound pride for Fred. He knew that he and the rest of the 442nd had paved the way to that place. Watching his parents raise their hands at their swearing-in ceremony, he thought to himself, *By God, you had a piece of this*.[71]

There were multiple efforts to persuade the government to formally apologize for the incarcerations and to pay compensation to the families who had been affected. In 1983, a federal commission recommended that Congress and the president issue an apology, establish a foundation to educate the American people on this hidden part of their history, and pay each surviving detainee twenty thousand dollars in compensation.

Rudy Tokiwa and dozens of 442nd veterans went to Washington, DC, to meet with senators and members of Congress, pressing them to enact the recommendations into law. Finally, in August 1988, after initially opposing the legislation, President Ronald Reagan signed the Civil Liberties Act, which declared that the incarcerations of Japanese Americans were "carried out without adequate security reasons and without any acts of espionage or sabotage, and were motivated largely by racial prejudice, wartime hysteria, and a failure of political leadership."[72]

★ ★ ★ ★

Gordon Hirabayashi was released from federal prison and reunited with Esther and their children shortly after the war ended. For the rest of his life, he continued to speak out in defense of civil rights for all Americans. He died early in 2012.

Later that year, President Barack Obama posthumously conferred on him the Presidential Medal of Freedom, the highest civilian honor an American can win. As he presented the medal at the White House, President Obama quoted Gordon's own words, stating the one simple principle for which Gordon fought: "Unless citizens are willing to stand up for the Constitution, it's not worth the paper it's written on."[73]

A FINAL WORD

THE SOLDIERS OF THE 442ND Regimental Combat Team won more medals and more honors than any other unit of its size and length of service in American military history. Those honors came at a terrible cost. Both the men of the 442nd and their brothers in the 100th Infantry Battalion suffered an extraordinarily high level of casualties throughout World War II. The 100th, in fact, became known early in the war as the "Purple Heart Battalion" because they were awarded so many Purple Heart medals for the injuries they had suffered.

Although they aren't discussed in this book, it's also important to note that in addition to those who served in the 442nd and the 100th, hundreds of Japanese Americans served in the US Army's Military Intelligence Service, where they used their Japanese-language skills to listen in on enemy radio transmissions and interrogate Japanese prisoners of war. In many cases, these soldiers served in combat alongside other army units, and a number of them gave their lives performing this role.

Looking back on the enormous sacrifices made by

Japanese Americans during World War II, I think we have to ask ourselves some questions. Were those sacrifices worthwhile for Japanese Americans? Did they finally put an end to the kind of racism that Fred, Rudy, Kats, Gordon, and thousands of other Japanese Americans experienced before the war?

The answer, sadly, is mixed. Certainly, many Japanese American families have forged successful and happy lives in America since World War II. For the most part, they have not experienced the same relentless barrages of open racism as the Nisei soldiers and their families did. Most Americans now recognize that hateful words like "Jap" have no place in our society. But, looking back on the stories told in this book, I think it's important to end by underscoring that racism is still an everyday concern for millions of Asians living in America.

When Chinese immigrants first came to the United States in the 1840s, many of them were met with hatred and outright violence. Their homes were burned, they were beaten and robbed, and vicious name-calling followed them wherever they went. Prominent politicians and ordinary Americans called them "rats" and "snakes" and "locusts." The same voices falsely accused the Chinese immigrants of bringing disease and plagues to the country. Newspapers and Hollywood movies spread these false ideas and promoted what they called the Yellow Peril—the false notion that

Chinese and other Asian immigrants were threatening to destroy America. These racist ideas became so prevalent that in 1882 and 1924 Congress passed laws first limiting and then completely banning the immigration of Asians to the United States—a ban based entirely on race.

Then, in the years before, during, and immediately after World War II, the same false claims that had been directed at Chinese immigrants were directed at Japanese immigrants and at their American children. They, too, were compared to pests like rats, snakes, and locusts. They, too, were accused of bringing disease and plague to the United States. They were told there were neighborhoods where they could not live. They were banned from public places, like swimming pools and ice rinks. And, finally, when the war came, they were forced from their homes and incarcerated in the camps you have read about in this book, even as their sons were fighting for the United States.

In recent years, sadly, we have seen some of the same racist language and hateful ideas that were directed at Chinese and Japanese immigrants earlier in our history now being directed against newer Asian immigrants as well as Americans of Asian ancestry. Once again, we have seen politicians and media figures digging up the old lies, associating Asians with pests and bringers of disease. Once again, acts of violence have been leveled against Asians in America, simply because of their race.

So, as you think about the stories of Gordon, Kats, Rudy, and Fred, I hope you will remember that their stories aren't just history. Their stories shine a light on our own time. They remind us that there is still much work to be done in the business of creating a society free of the kinds of racism they and their families faced. And their stories do something more. They remind us also what it means to be a good American. They show us how four good-hearted young Americans who believed deeply in their country rose to meet the desperate challenges of their time. They give faces and names to the kinds of courage, conscience, and principle that define us as Americans when we are at our best. In short, they inspire us to do as well as they did, to be as good as they were. That is their gift to us.

ACKNOWLEDGMENTS

AS MANY BOOKS ARE, THIS one was ushered into the world with the help of many people.

First and foremost, I want to thank Tom Ikeda of the Denshō project in Seattle. It was largely through my early conversations with Tom that I came to fully understand how important it is for all of us—particularly in these times we are living through—to better understand the experience of Japanese Americans before and during World War II. In addition to the astounding collection of oral histories, letters, newspapers, photographs, and other material that Tom has made available to the world on the Denshō website, he provided invaluable guidance and advice. I also want to thank the staff at Denshō—particularly Brian Niiya, Denshō's excellent historian—for all the help they have given me in making good use of the resources they tirelessly collect and curate.

I am particularly indebted also to Fred Shiosaki, as well as the family members of some of the other young men whose lives I chronicle in the book—Michael Shiosaki, Mariko Miho, Judy Niizawa, and Robin Tokiwa. Thank you all so much for entrusting me with your loved ones' amazing stories. I can only hope that I have done some small measure of justice to them.

Among the many people in Hawai'i who contributed in so many ways, my thanks go out to Leilani Dawson at the

University of Hawai'i Manoa; Michiko Kodama-Nishimoto; Gwen Fujie; Shari Y. Tamashiro; and two remarkable gentlemen—Flint Yonashiro and Roy Fujii—both veterans of the 552nd's B Battery.

On the mainland, special thanks to Janet and Jim Ohta; David Takami; L. Stuart Hirai; Jamie Henricks, Kristen Hayashi, and Anne Burroughs at the Japanese American National Museum; Judy Willman; and Kiyomi Hayashi, for all things Quaker and for keeping me ever in the light.

In the world of book publishing, I can never think of words superlative enough to express again my deep, heartfelt gratitude to two tough, warm, ferociously brilliant women—my agent at WME, Dorian Karchmar, and my editor at Viking, Wendy Wolf. And for this young reader's edition of the book, I offer my hearty thanks to Liz Hudson for a wonderful job doing the heavy lifting of creating the adaptation, and to Kelsey Murphy for her excellent advice and keeping us on course throughout.

And finally, at home, I have yet again been blessed by the love and encouragement of my family—my daughters Emily and Robin and my wife, Sharon. On this particular journey, Sharon has been with me every step of the way, lending me her keen insights, her excellent editorial eye, and her terrific instincts for good storytelling. More than ever, without her there would be no books.

RESOURCES

WEBSITES

"Archives Spotlight: Remembering Nisei Veterans." Denshō
Catalyst: https://densho.org/catalyst/archives-spotlight
-remembering-nisei-veterans/

Go for Broke National Education Center: GoForBroke.org

The Hawai'i Nisei Story website: https://web.archive.org
/web/20220418002323/http://nisei.hawaii.edu/page
/home

United States Holocaust Memorial Museum: USHMM.org

INTERVIEWS AND ARCHIVES

Clark, General Mark, letter to Colonel Charles Wilbur
Pence. September 7, 1944. https://ddr.densho.org
/media/ddr-csujad-1/ddr-csujad-1-200-mezzanine
-d2081380e8.pdf.

Congressional Record, December 15, 1941.

Futamase, Fumi Tokiwa, interview by Judy Niizawa. 1995.

Higuchi, Hiro, letters to his wife. University of Hawai'i Special Collections, Hamilton Library.

Hirabayashi, Gordon, Denshō interviews. April 1999–May
2000. Denshō Digital Repository.

Hirabayashi, Gordon, interview by Lois Horn. 1990.

Inouye, Daniel, Denshō interview by Tom Ikeda and Beverly
Kashin. Americans of Japanese Ancestry Veterans National

Convention, Honolulu, June 30, 1998. Denshō Digital
Repository.

Miho, Kats, interview by Michi Kodama-Nishimoto and
Warren Nishimoto. November 16, 1989.

Niizawa, Judy, interview by Daniel J. Brown. March 17,
2017.

Shiosaki, Fred, Denshō interview by Tom Ikeda. April 26
and 27, 2006. Denshō Digital Repository.

Shiosaki, Fred, interviews by Daniel J. Brown. April 10 and
July 2, 2016.

Tokiwa, Rudy, Denshō interview by Tom Ikeda. Americans
of Japanese Ancestry Veterans National Convention, Honolulu, July 2 and 3, 1998. Denshō Digital Repository.

Tokiwa, Rudy, interview by Ian Kawata. June 3, 2001. Go
for Broke National Education Center Oral History Project.
Japanese American Military History Collective.

Tsukiyama Papers. University of Hawai'i Special Collections,
Hamilton Library.

NOTES

1 Steven M. Gillon, *Pearl Harbor: FDR Leads the Nation into War* (New York: Basic Books, 2011), 13.

2 Lyn Crost, *Honor by Fire: Japanese Americans at War in Europe and the Pacific* (Novato, CA: Presidio Press, 1994), 9; Ted Tsukiyama, panelist, 70th anniversary Pearl Harbor symposium, broadcast on *American History TV*, C-SPAN, December 5, 2011.

3 Daniel Inouye, interview by Christine Sato, August 14, 2000, Go for Broke National Education Center Oral History Project, transcript, Japanese American Military History Collective, https://ndajams.omeka.net/items/show/1053156.

4 Katsugo Miho, interview by Michi Kodama-Nishimoto and Warren Nishimoto, November 16, 1989, and Kats Miho's compiled narrative on the Hawai'i Nisei Story website.

5 Katsugo Miho, 1989 interview by the Nishimotos.

6 Thelma Chang, *"I Can Never Forget": Men of the 100th/442nd* (Honolulu: Sigi Productions, 1991), 84.

7 John C. Hughes, "Fred Shiosaki: The Rescue of the Lost Battalion" (Olympia: Legacy Washington, Office of Secretary of State, 2015), 1.

8 Time–Life–Fortune News Bureau, *War Comes to the U.S.—Dec. 7, 1941: The First 30 Hours as Reported from the U.S. and Abroad* (Norwalk, CT: Easton Press, 2014), 333.

9   Time–Life–Fortune News Bureau, *War*, 441.

10 Fred Shiosaki, interview by Tom Ikeda, April 26 and 27, 2006, Denshō Digital Repository.

11 Fumiye Miho, unpublished, untitled memoir.

12 Richard Reeves, *Infamy: The Shocking Story of the Japanese-American Internment in World War II* (New York: Henry Holt, 2015), 34.

13 Reeves, *Infamy*, 19.

14 Katsugo Mijo, interview by Michi Kodama-Nishimoto and Warren Nishimoto, February 16, 2006, Denshō Digital Repository.

15 Rudy Tokiwa, interview by Tom Ikeda and Judy Niizawa, Americans of Japanese Ancestry Veterans National Convention, Honolulu, July 2 and 3, 1998, Denshō Digital Repository; and interview by Ian Kawata, June 3, 2001, Go for Broke National Education Center Oral History Project, Japanese American Military History Collective.

16 Rudy Tokiwa, 1998 Denshō interview by Tom Ikeda and 2001 Go for Broke National Education Center interview by Ian Kawata. Many other details come from Daniel J. Brown's interview with Rudy's partner, Judy Niizawa, on March 17, 2017.

17 *Congressional Record* (December 15, 1941).

18 Reeves, *Infamy*, 7.

19 Rudy Tokiwa, 1998 Denshō interview by Tom Ikeda; Fumi Tokiwa Futamase, interview by Judy Niizawa, 1995; Judy

Niizawa, interview by Daniel J. Brown, March 17, 2017.

20 "California U's Best Student is in Jap Camp." *Seattle Times*, May 13, 1942, A1.

21 My portrait of Gordon is drawn from three principal sources: a series of interviews with Denshō between April 1999 and May 2000, a 1990 interview by Lois Horn, and his own account in Gordon K. Hirabayashi, *A Principled Stand: The Story of Hirabayashi v. United States* (Seattle: University of Washington Press, 2013), 127.

22 Hirabayashi, *A Principled Stand*, 61–62.

23 Rudy Tokiwa, 2001 Go for Broke National Education Center interview by Ian Kawata.

24 Hirabayashi, *A Principled Stand*, 120–26.

25 Fred Shiosaki, 2006 Denshō interview by Tom Ikeda.

26 Roosevelt's memo to Secretary Stimson, February 1, 1943, a copy of which can also be found in the Tsuki-yama Papers, University of Hawai'i Special Collections, Hamilton Library. Although often attributed to FDR himself, the memo was authored by Elmer Davis, who ran the Office of War Information.

27 Fred Shiosaki, 2006 Denshō interview by Tom Ikeda.

28 Katsugo Miho, interview by Warren Nishimoto, n.d.

29 "2600 New U.S. Soldiers Get Public Aloha," *Honolulu Star-Bulletin*, March 29, 1943.

30 Daniel Inouye, interview by Tom Ikeda and Beverly Kashino, Americans of Japanese Ancestry Veterans

National Convention, Honolulu, June 30, 1998, Denshō Digital Repository.

31 Rudy Tokiwa, 2011 Go for Broke National Education Center Interview by Ian Kawata.

32 Hirabayashi, *A Principled Stand*, 139.

33 Gordon Hirabayashi, interview by Tom Ikeda and Alice Ito, May 4, 2000, Denshō Digital Repository.

34 Hirabayashi, *A Principled Stand*, 134.

35 Hirabayashi, *A Principled Stand*, 145

36 Hirabayashi, *A Principled Stand*,148–149

37 "442nd's First C.O." Newspaper clipping from an unknown publication.

38 John Terry, *With Hawaii's AJA Boys at Camp Shelby, Mississippi* (Honolulu: Honolulu Star-Bulletin, Ltd., 1943), 25.

39 Rudy Tokiwa, 1998 Denshō interview by Tom Ikeda and Judy Niizawa.

40 James M. McCaffrey, *Going for Broke: Japanese American Soldiers in the War against Nazi Germany* (Norman: University of Oklahoma Press, 2013), 177.

41 "Nisei Rejects Draft Board's Questionnaire," *The Seattle Times*, February 15, 1944.

42 "'I Love Him,' Says Bride of Japanese-American." Undated newspaper clipping.

43 "White Girl Weds Japanese Youth," *Reno Gazette News*, August 2, 1944.

44 Gordon Hirabayashi, interview by Tom Ikeda, February

12, 2000, Denshō Digital Repository.

45 Gordon talks about the anonymous hate mail and the fifty-dollar gift in his 2000 Denshō interview.

46 Eric L. Muller, *Free to Die for Their Country: The Story of the Japanese American Draft Resisters in World War II* (Chicago: University of Chicago Press, 2001), 104.

47 Muller, *Free to Die for Their Country*, 143.

48 Rudy Tokiwa, 1998 Denshō interview by Tom Ikeda and Judy Niizawa.

49 Hiro Higuchi to his wife, July 8, 1944. The letters were donated to the University of Hawai'i by their daughter Jane and are archived in the Special Collections at the Hamilton Library.

50 Rudy Tokiwa mentions the villagers thinking the Nisei must be Chinese in his 1998 Denshō interview and talks about them greeting the Nisei soldiers with kisses in his 2001 Go for Broke National Education Center interview.

51 The incidents surrounding the awakening of first the Second Battalion and then the Third are related in Orville C. Shirey, *Americans: The Story of the 442nd Combat Team* (Washington, DC: Washington Infantry Journal Press, 1946), 58–63.

52 The conversation involving Rudy, Pursall, and Dahlquist is drawn from Rudy's accounts given in his 1998 Denshō interview and his Go for Broke Education Center interview on March 24, 2002.

53 This exchange is drawn from Rudy Tokiwa's 1998 Denshō interview.

54 McCaffrey, *Going for Broke*, 266.

55 Scott McGaugh, *Honor Before Glory: The Epic World War II Story of the Japanese American GIs Who Rescued the Lost Battalion* (Boston: Da Capo Press, 2016), 158.

56 Fred Shiosaki, 2006 Denshō interview by Tom Ikeda.

57 Fred's account is largely drawn from my interviews with him on April 10 and July 2, 2016, as well as his 2006 Denshō interview with Tom Ikeda.

58 Pierre Moulin, *U.S. Samuraïs in Bruyères: People of France and Japanese Americans: Incredible Story* (France: Peace & Freedom Trail, 1993), 108. Translated from the original French edition, *U.S. samuraïs en Lorraine* (Vagney, France: Gérard Louis, 1988).

59 "Wounded Nisei Reported Shoved Out of Shop," *Los Angeles Times*, November 11, 1944; "Wounded Nisei War Veteran Ejected from Barber Shop," *Pacific Citizen*, November 18, 1944.

60 Rudy Tokiwa, 1998 Denshō interview.

61 Daniel Inouye, 1998 Denshō interview.

62 General Mark Clark to Colonel Charles Wilbur Pence on September 7, 1944. A copy of this letter can be found on the Denshō website at https://ddr.densho.org/media /ddr-csujad-1/ddr-csujad-1-200-mezzanine-d2081380e8.pdf.

63 Solly Ganor, *Light One Candle* (New York: Kodansha International, 1995), 346–347.

64 Solly Ganor, interview with the United States Holocaust Memorial Museum, April 27, 1993.

65 *Tampa Times*, May 7, 1945.

66 Recounted in a letter from Hiro Higuchi to his wife on May 8, 1945, and in Loni Ding's film *Nisei Soldier: Standard Bearer for an Exiled People*, Center for Asian American Media, 1984.

67 Fred described his reaction to the end of the war both in my interview with him on April 10, 2016, as well as his 2006 Denshō interview.

68 Fred Shiosaki, 2006 Denshō interview by Tom Ikeda.

69 Rudy Tokiwa, 1998 Denshō interview with Tom Ikeda and Judy Niizawa.

70 Rudy Tokiwa, 2002 Go for Broke National Education Center interview.

71 Hughes, "Fred Shiosaki: The Rescue of the Lost Battalion."

72 The language is from the act itself, as quoted in Sharon Yamato, "Civil Liberties Act of 1988," Densho Encyclopedia, updated August 24, 2020, https://encyclopedia.densho.org/Civil_Liberties_Act_of_1988.

73 Medal of Freedom Ceremony, May 29, 2012, transcript, C-SPAN, https://www.c-span.org/video/cc/?progid=278268.

SELECTED BIBLIOGRAPHY

Crost, Lyn. *Honor by Fire: Japanese Americans at War in Europe and the Pacific.* Novato, CA: Presidio Press, 1994.

Ding, Loni, director. *Nisei Soldier: Standard Bearer for an Exiled People.* Center for Asian American Media, 1984.

Hirabayashi, Gordon K. *A Principled Stand: The Story of Hirabayashi v. United States.* Seattle: University of Washington Press, 2013.

"'I Love Him,' Says Bride of Japanese-American." Undated newspaper clipping.

McCaffrey, James M. *Going for Broke: Japanese American Soldiers in the War against Nazi Germany.* Norman: University of Oklahoma Press, 2013.

McGaugh, Scott. *Honor before Glory: The Epic World War II Story of the Japanese American GIs Who Rescued the Lost Battalion.* Boston: Da Capo Press, 2016.

Moulin, Pierre. *US Samuraïs in Bruyères.* France: Peace & Freedom Trail, 1993. Translated edition of *U.S. samuraïs en Lorraine* (Vagney, France: Gérard Louis, 1988).

Muller, Eric L. *Free to Die for Their Country: The Story of the Japanese American Draft Resisters in World War II.* Chicago: University of Chicago Press, 2001.

"Nisei Rejects Draft Board's Questionnaire." *The Seattle Times,* February 15, 1944.

Reeves, Richard. *Infamy: The Shocking Story of the Japanese-American Internment in World War II*. New York: Henry Holt, 2015.

Shirey, Orville C. *Americans: The Story of the 442nd Combat Team*. Washington, DC: Washington Infantry Journal Press, 1946.

Terry, John. *With Hawaii's AJA Boys at Camp Shelby, Mississippi*. Honolulu: Honolulu Star-Bulletin, Ltd. 1943.

"Wounded Nisei Reported Shoved Out of Shop." *Los Angeles Times*, November 11, 1944.

"Wounded Nisei War Veteran Ejected from Barber Shop." *Pacific Citizen*, November 18, 1944.

PHOTO CREDITS

Page 72, Courtesy of Library of Congress.

Page 75, Courtesy of the Tokiwa Family Collection.

Page 77, Source: Shiosaki Family Collection.

Page 90, Source: Critical Past.

Page 112, Source: Bettmann via Getty Images.

Page 119, Map. Credit: Jeffrey L. Ward

Page 135, Courtesy of the Seattle Nisei Veterans Committee Collection and the US Army.

Page 137, Courtesy of the National Archives and Records Administration.

Page 138, Courtesy of the National Archives and Records Administration.

Page 142, Map. Credit: Jeffrey L. Ward

Page 146, Source: Critical Past.

Page 148, Source: Katsugo Miho Family Estate.

Page 153, Courtesy of the National Archives and Records Administration.

Page 161, Courtesy of the National Archives and Records Administration.

Page 172, Map. Credit: Jeffrey L. Ward

Page 182, Map. Credit: Jeffrey L. Ward

Page 193, Source: US Army Signal Corps/Hawaii War Records Depository.

Page 199, Courtesy of the National Archives and Records Administration.

INDEX

Note: Italicized page numbers indicate
material in tables or illustrations.

FOR ANOTHER THRILLING NONFICTION TALE FROM DANIEL JAMES BROWN, READ

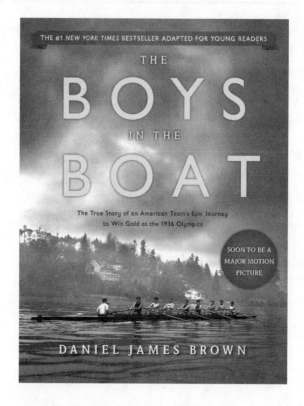

The #1 *New York Times* bestselling story about the American Olympic rowing triumph in Nazi Germany